SIMPLY BEAUTIFUL DRESDENS

Create 18 Quilts With One Template

by MISSOURI STAR QUILT CO.

EXECUTIVE EDITOR
Natalie Earnheart

CREATIVE TEAM
Jenny Doan, Natalie Earnheart, Misty Doan, Christine Ricks, Grant Flook, Mike Brunner, Lauren Dorton, Jennifer Dowling, Dustin Weant, Jessica Toye, Kimberly Forman, Denise Lane

EDITOR & COPYWRITER
Nichole Spravzoff, Liz Gubernatis, Kevin Gubernatis, Lindsay Conner

SEWIST TEAM
Jenny Doan, Natalie Earnheart, Misty Doan, Courtenay Hughes, Carol Henderson, Janice Richardson, Cathleen Tripp

ADDITIONAL PHOTOGRAPHY
Derek Israelsen Studio, Salt Lake City, UT

PRINTING COORDINATOR
Rob Stoebener

PRINTING SERVICES
Frederic Printing
14701 East 38th Avenue, Aurora, CO

CONTACT US
Missouri Star Quilt Company
114 N Davis
Hamilton, MO 64644
888-571-1122
info@missouriquiltco.com

Simply Beautiful Dresdens: Create 18 Quilts With One Template by Missouri Star Quilt Co. ©2022. All Rights Reserved by Missouri Star Quilt Company. Reproduction in whole or in part in any language without written permission from Missouri Star Quilt Company or Simply Beautiful Dresdens: Create 18 Quilts With One Template is prohibited. No one may copy, reprint, or distribute any of the patterns or materials in this book for commercial use without written permission of Missouri Star Quilt Company. Anything you make using our patterns or ideas, it's yours!

ARTICLES

08
DISCOVER SIMPLY BEAUTIFUL DRESDENS
An introduction from Jenny Doan.

10
HOW TO CREATE A QUILT
Step-by-step tips from start to finish.

20
USING PRECUTS
Make quilting easier than ever before!

22
PUT YOUR OWN SPIN ON IT
Find a circle for the center of your Dresden plates!

ARTICLES

88
ALL ABOUT DRESDEN APPLIQUÉ
How to securely stitch Dresdens onto blocks.

150
MAKING DRESDEN BORDERS & STRIPS
Create a custom pieced border with Dresdens!

182
DRESDEN MAGIC TIPS & TRICKS
How to make shapes with Dresdens.

208
TEMPLATES

212
REFERENCE

PATTERNS

26 DRESDEN BOTANICA

34 MINI SUNFLOWER PILLOW

44 GRANDMOTHER'S FAN

52 HERE COMES THE SUN

60 FANCY DRESDEN FANS

68 TINY DRESDENS

76 TURKEY TROT

94 DRESDEN TREE WALL HANGING

SEW ALONG WITH MSQC!

Scan this code with your phone or device for Digital Extras! *(You will need to be connected to the internet to do this.)*

1. Open your camera app.
2. Select the rear-facing camera in Photo mode. (No selfies here!)
3. Center the QR code to the right on your screen.
4. Hold your phone/device steady for a couple of seconds.
5. Tap the notification that pops up to open the link.

PATTERNS

104
DRESDEN WREATH WALL HANGING

112
BLOOM AND GROW WALL HANGING

124
SPRING DRESDENS TABLE RUNNER

134
JOSH'S STAR

142
DRESDEN COIN

154
DRESDEN SQUARED TABLE RUNNER

164
CHECKERED DRESDEN BED RUNNER

172
IMPROV DRESDEN GEESE TABLE RUNNER

188
ALL IN A ROLL & ALL IN A ROW PILLOWS

198
SPARE CHANGE BAG

DISCOVER SIMPLY BEAUTIFUL DRESDENS

Dresden quilts and all the shapes you can make with Dresden blades really inspire me. I love playing "What if?" with fans of Dresdens! Whether it's finding an easy way to make a traditional, heirloom-style quilt or a fun wall hanging for a favorite holiday, I just love seeing Dresden blocks turn into something simply beautiful!

When did you first decide to make a Dresden quilt? My love of Dresdens began long ago, when we first opened up shop back in 2008. We had one longarm machine and would finish people's quilts for them as the main source of our livelihood. Our friends and neighbors tried their best to support us, but most weren't even quilters. Thankfully, many of them had held onto unfinished quilt tops their ancestors had made, tucked away in storage closets and cedar chests. It was such a special privilege to transform quilt tops from generations past into finished quilts that, after years of waiting, could finally be used and enjoyed.

A good number of those vintage quilt tops were Dresden Plates, and I just couldn't get over how beautiful they were. I absolutely fell in love with those beautiful little petals with perfect points, but I was too intimidated to try and create one myself. I think one of the reasons I became so smitten with them was I never thought I would have one, let alone make one.

When I finally gathered up the courage, I decided to make my very own Dresden Plate quilt out of reproduction 1930's fabric, and was delighted to discover how simple it actually was. With just a little ingenuity, a special ruler, and a charm pack, my first Dresden Plate block came together quickly—and many more have followed since then! If you want something enough, it is possible and you can do it one seam at a time.

Since my first Dresden Plate quilt, I've become obsessed with Dresdens and I see them everywhere! One year I made a Thanksgiving turkey with Dresden feathers, then I made a Christmas tree hanging with green Dresden branches. I've also made several spring wall hangings with Dresden flowers and I've even created cute bags, purses, and pillows from Dresdens. Inside this book you'll discover a collection of my favorite Dresden patterns. We've also included tips and techniques to help you learn to play "What if?" with your Dresdens and I'm excited to share all I've discovered with you. Altogether, there are 18 projects you can make with a little ingenuity, a single ruler, and your favorite fabrics.

One of the great joys of quilting is knowing that we are creating heirlooms that will be cherished and enjoyed long after this moment has become a distant memory. Take time to learn something new and you'll leave a lasting legacy.

JENNY DOAN
MISSOURI STAR QUILT CO.

HOW TO CREATE A QUILT

Congratulations on taking the next step in your quilting journey! If you're reading this, you're already on your way to honing new skills that will have you creating beautiful, timeless Dresden quilts and projects. We are excited to walk with you through this rewarding creative hobby—and what better way to start than with some quilting basics! There is so much to learn from each step in the process, from measuring and cutting to quilting and binding.

The patterns in this book are well-suited to beginning quilters as well as those who have some experience with piecing and appliqué. While there's no single "right way" to make a quilt, we want to get you quickly on the path to success. You can even bookmark this section for reference later on. We can't wait to see your finished projects! Don't forget to share them with us by tagging #msqcshowandtell on social media.

NEED A 90 SECOND VIDEO HOW-TO?

Open Camera, Scan Code, Watch our Dresden Block Quilt Snips Video!

cutting fabric

Are you ready to learn the best tools for cutting up quilting fabric?

A self-healing cutting mat is the first item you'll need for cutting fabric. We recommend getting a large 36" x 24" mat if you have the space for it! Smaller mats are great for traveling with.

Note: We know it's tempting to press blocks after trimming them on a cutting mat, but resist the urge! We don't want yours to warp and get bent out of shape.

A good rotary cutter (45mm size) is also a must. Many different types are available, some with ergonomic handles and others for lefties. Don't forget to pick up a few extra blades to sub in when your old loses its sharpness. Changing blades also helps extend the life of your cutting mat. We recommend investing in a 6" x 24" acrylic ruler for cutting yardage or a smaller size like 6" x 12" for slicing up precuts. There are many sizes of rulers, but you'll find yourself going to these particular ones again and again.

Cutting fabric with a rotary cutter can be incredibly efficient because you can stack precuts and slice a few layers at a time. To set up your cutting station, first place the mat on a desk or table at a comfortable standing height. Keep your ruler handy and remember to keep the rotary blade closed and locked when not in use. The grid lines on your cutting mat and ruler will help you line up your fabric and cut nice, straight lines. Starting with the rotary cutter close to your body, press the blade down flush with the edge of the ruler. Slowly and steadily cut in the direction away from your body, holding the ruler firmly with your non-dominant hand but keeping your fingers safely out of the way.

piecing & appliqué

After the fabrics are cut, it's time to get piecing! Want to avoid skipped stitches? Put in a fresh 80/12 size universal quilting needle before starting a new project, or after about 8 hours of sewing. Also make sure you're using quality thread, such as a 50 weight cotton, for piecing. Vintage spools are great for nostalgia, but the thread tends to break easily—better to pick up some new threads in neutral colors like white, grey, and cream.

It's a good practice to use a consistent ¼" seam in all of your quilting projects. Some sewing machines come with a ¼" foot to help you keep a consistent seam allowance.

Tip: If you don't have one of these handy feet, you can apply a piece of masking or washi tape to the needle plate marking ¼" from the needle when it's centered.

Because we are working with Dresdens in this book, you'll also get to add another trick to your quilting toolbox—appliqué. This is how you'll stitch down pointy ends on your Dresden blades and attach circles to cover raw edges. See *All About Dresden Appliqué* on page 88 for a rundown on our favorite appliqué tools and methods, and *Put Your Own Spin on It* on page 22 for more on finding and creating the perfect circle templates for your projects.

pressing & trimming blocks

So, you've got all your quilt blocks sewn and arranged into rows. It's almost time to sew them together. Before you make a quilt top, we recommend pressing the seams of each block to get a crisp and clean finish—after all, you'll want to cement all that hard work you did with piecing! If you are working with both light and dark fabrics, press the seams toward the darker fabric for the best results.

After pressing, it's time to trim the edges or "square up" the quilt blocks. Square-shaped rulers are available in different sizes to help with this task. **Tip:** If you don't have a square ruler, you can line up diagonal seams on your block with at the 45° mark on your long ruler before trimming off that extra little bit of fabric.

As you sew blocks together into rows, they will fit happily together as long as you nest the seams. To do this, press one row of seams to the right and the next row of seams to the left. To join the rows, pin or clip them together at the seams. They should sew together snugly, creating less bulk.

After the last row is pieced together, you've got a quilt top! Press the quilt top, using some spray starch if you want to make it extra flat. Then trim and square up the entire top with a rotary cutter and the largest ruler you can find.

backing

Who says a quilt back can't be as pretty as the front? So many beautiful fabrics are available, and picking a bold print can help hide quilting mistakes better than solids. To prepare the backing fabric, measure the length and width of your quilt top, adding an extra 8 inches to both measurements if it's going to be machine quilted. The 108" wide backing fabrics work best for larger projects, or you can piece together 42" wide yardage to get the backing size you need.

Now, let's join the backing pieces together! First trim off the selvages (the stiff edges, sometimes with words) and use a ½" seam allowance to join the sections. Sew the fabrics together along the cut edge. To get less bulk, we like to press this seam open, rather than to one side. For small quilts (under 60" wide), you can place this backing seam horizontally, but vertical seams work better for larger quilts.

batting

Although batting isn't as pretty as quilting fabric, it can still be pretty fun to shop for! If you want your finished quilt to last through the years and hold up through many washes and trips through the dryer, we suggest choosing a high-quality cotton batting or 80/20 cotton-polyester blend. Battings can be purchased by the yard but are often conveniently prepackaged by quilt size.

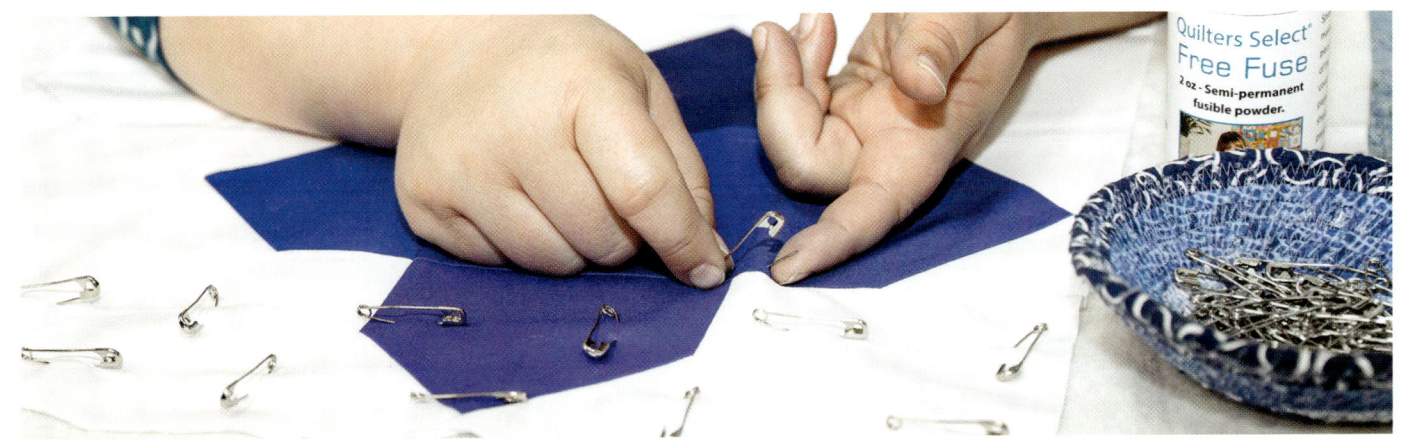

basting

Once you have the three layers of the "quilt sandwich" together (quilt top, batting, and backing), it's time for basting! In this step, you'll smooth out each layer and temporarily attach them in preparation for quilting. Basting spray is a good choice for small projects, and you can't go wrong with safety pins for larger quilts. Placing the pins every few inches will keep the layer locked as you quilt. Want to skip this step altogether? Hire a longarm quilter and they will feed your quilt top, batting, and backing right onto the quilt frame, so no basting is necessary.

quilting

The quilting designs you choose can be a reflection of your personality and also make a big difference on the look and texture of your finished quilt. Beginners may want to sew directly on the major seams, which is "called stitching in the ditch". Another option is to choose a freemotion quilting design like loops, wavy lines, or bubbles. This trick helps move the eye away from the piecing, in effect disguising any seams that didn't line up quite right. Voila!

When quilting a Dresden plate or fan, it's often nice to quilt only around the edges and along straight lines. When you leave decorative quilting to the background, it really helps the appliqué pop. Timid quilters and beginners may want to choose a thread that matches the quilt top's background. White, off-white, or grey can blend well with all kinds of fabrics. If your backing fabric is dark, you can use a darker thread in the bobbin and feed a lighter color thread through the machine. There are no rules when it comes to thread color, so feel free to be as bold as you'd like!

binding

After you've quilted your project and trimmed off the excess batting and backing, it's time to finish your quilt with binding! Quilt binding can be purchased in readymade packs, or you can create your own from yardage (cut from selvedge to selvedge) or 2½" jelly roll strips. We've listed the yardage needed for binding on all of the Dresden projects in this book.

machine binding

You'll find that seasoned quilters have their favorite ways to bind a quilt. We suggest machine stitching the binding to the front of the quilt and hand sewing it to the back with an invisible slip stitch.

Start the binding in the middle of a long edge of the quilt (not at the corner) and leave a 10" tail of loose binding when you start sewing. Use a walking foot to sew the binding to the quilt ¼" from the edge.

joining strips – plus sign method

We're almost there! To join binding strips together, lay one strip end across the other strip end with the right sides together, like a plus sign. Stitch from the top inside to the bottom outside corners crossing the intersections of fabric as you sew. Trim the seam to ¼" and press the center seam open to reduce bulk. Join as many strips together as you need to equal the perimeter of the quilt (the sum of all the edges) plus about 15" to 20" inches more to finish. The last step is to press the long strip in half widthwise to hide those seams, and you're ready to start binding your quilt!

mitered corners

Ready to make perfect mitered corners every time? When you are ¼" from a corner, stop sewing and backstitch once. Lift the presser foot, remove the quilt, and clip your threads. Flip the binding up at a 90° angle to the edge just sewn, making a tiny triangle. The binding tail will point straight up. Next, fold the binding back down from the top edge, right next to the side that will be sewn next, aligning the raw edges. Sew from the top fold down on the next side, doing a little backstitch right at the beginning.

We're almost there! To join binding strips together, lay one strip end across the other strip end with the right sides together, like a plus sign. Stitch from the top inside to the bottom outside corners crossing the intersections of fabric as you sew. Trim the seam to ¼" and press the center seam open to reduce bulk. Join as many strips together as you need to equal the perimeter of the quilt (the sum of all the edges) plus about 15" to 20" inches more to finish. The last step is to press the long strip in half widthwise to hide those seams, and you're ready to start binding your quilt!

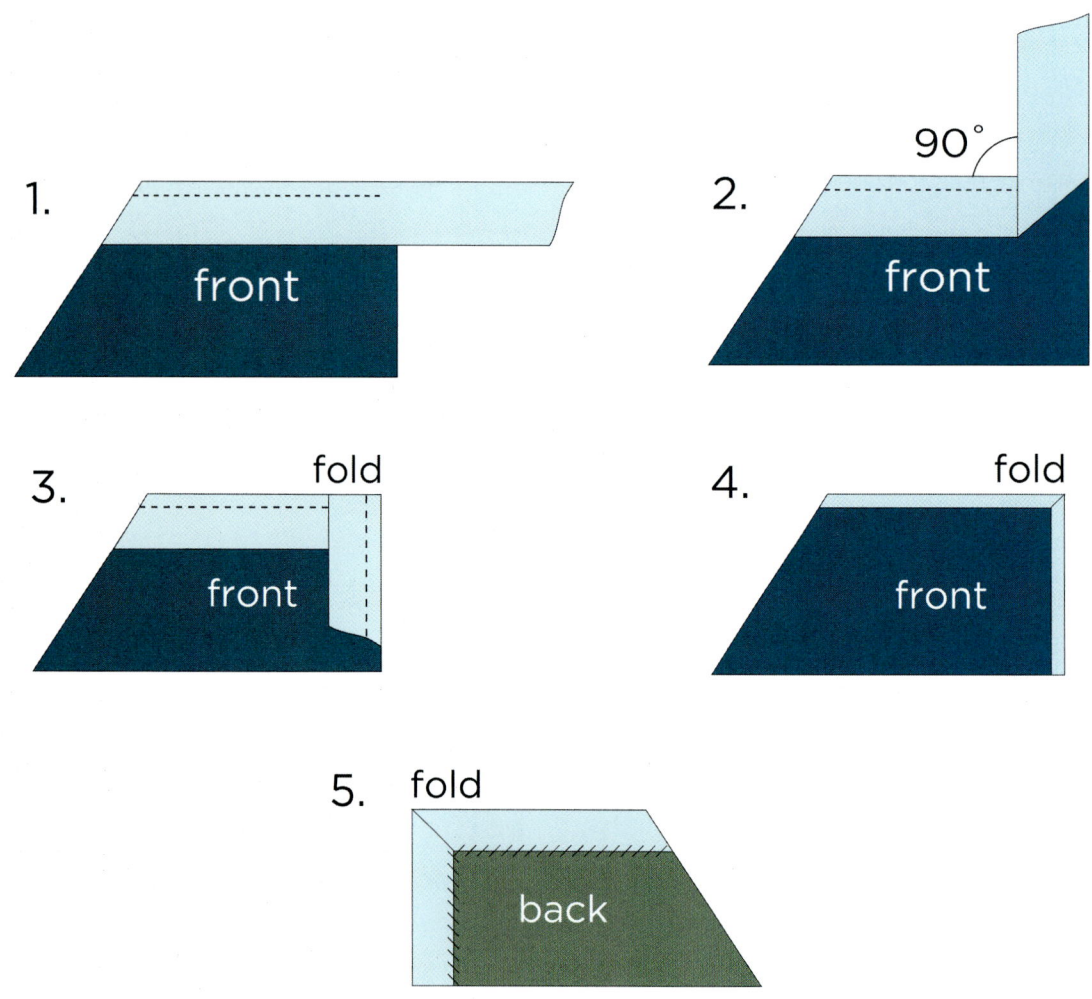

close the binding

Stop sewing when your needle is 12" away from the starting point. Take the 10" binding tails you've left at both ends. Lay them so they overlap each other and press a crease at their meeting point. Fold back the extra, measuring just 2½" inches of overlap. Trim off the rest of the binding strip and set it aside.

Use the plus sign method to match the edges and pin in place. Use a pencil or washable pen to mark your sewing line and stitch a straight line from the top inside corner to the bottom outside corner. After you press the seam open and fold the entire section of binding in half, it should rest neatly against the edge of your quilt. Stitch that section to the front side of your quilt, flip the edge over to the back side, and tack it in place with an invisible stitch or machine stitch.

USING PRECUTS

Here at Missouri Star Quilt Company, we're all about making quilting and sewing easier and more accessible than ever before and precuts are the best thing since sliced bread! Precut fabrics are packages of fabric that are cut to size in advance. There's no need to cut fabrics for hours; they help you get right to the good part without all the fuss. Almost every single Missouri Star pattern is made to be used with precut fabrics so all you need to know is how many precuts to choose of each size and you're good to go!

These Dresden projects are handpicked especially for precuts, along with a few tips and tricks to make sewing them together fast and fun. When you begin quilting with precut fabrics, it really couldn't be any easier. Keep on reading and learn how to make the most of each type of featured precut.

2½" PRECUT
JELLY ROLL

This is how we roll! Jelly rolls or 2½" strips are one of the most popular precuts out there for a reason. They look so cute all rolled up and they are incredibly useful. It's almost a shame to open them up for a project, but it's totally worth it. If you've ever spent a good amount of time trying to cut perfect strips, you know how valuable these rolls are! From the *Tiny Dresdens* (page 68) quilt to sashing and binding, 2½" strips get the job done. You can even slice them up into mini charms and use them to snowball corners and add cornerstones. There are just so many uses for these simple strips!

5" PRECUT
CHARM PACK

Prepare to be charmed! Charm packs are so cute and so easy to use. We like to keep them on hand for quick projects. Gather up a whole bunch of them and before you know it, they're quickly used right up without a single regret. These wonderful stacks of 5" squares can be used as-is for easy patchwork quilts or you cut them up into neat little quilt blocks that couldn't be simpler to create. One of our favorite 5" square quilts is *Bloom and Grow* on page 112 which uses each end of the Dresden template to make differently sized flowers from the same precut pack!

10" PRECUT
LAYER CAKE

Layer cakes sound so delicious, don't they? These lovely stacks of fabric help big, beautiful quilts come together in a snap! Whenever we get our hands on one, they don't last long. We can't help but cut into them and get right to the good part—sewing! These fantastic 10" squares are perfect for quilters who are just starting out because of their versatility. You can do so much with a simple square. For example, you can make both the *All in a Row and the All in a Roll Pillows* (page 188) from the same pack of 10" squares!

Put Your Own Spin On it

FINDING A CIRCLE FOR THE CENTER OF YOUR DRESDEN PLATE

It's time to talk about Dresden Plates! More specifically, it's time to talk about circle appliqués over Dresden Plates. Most traditional Dresden patterns call for an appliqué circle for the center of the Dresden Plate. If you want to be a little adventurous, you can search for your own circle. They are literally everywhere, you just need to know how and where to look!

DAISY OR SUNFLOWER?

First things first, before you can get going on your circle adventure, you have to choose your circle size. Now, there's no wrong answer, except one that doesn't fit with your vision. The circle you find doesn't have to be perfectly matched to our suggested sizes, but you'll need to have a general understanding of size to get started. Different patterns will suggest different center circle sizes, and bigger and smaller circle sizes will have a noticeable effect on the look of your project. Think about the difference between a daisy and a sunflower. You're going to want two very different circles depending on which of these you're trying to create.

AROUND THE ROOM

Once you've sorted out the size of circle you want, it's time to go on an adventure! Where do you start? Anywhere you like! First, in your sewing space, you'll find at least a couple of circles you could use.

Do you have a larger thread spool? It's base is a great size! Another great circle that we think is in most sewing rooms is a jelly roll still in the wrapping. It makes the perfect circle to trace, and what better reason to crack one open when you're done tracing it?

AROUND THE HOUSE

Not finding what you're looking for in your sewing space? Another great place to look for Dresden circles is just around the house. Those favorite candles—in or out of the jar—are often the perfect thing to use for a medium sized circle. Vases, rolls of tape, and circular based lamps are great choices too. You can also use any kind of compact disc, like a DVD, or Bluray. Say, then you could watch a movie while you finish up your Dresden project!

Quite possibly the absolute best place in your home to look for appliqué circle templates is the kitchen. Cups, bowls, plates, mugs, wine glasses, canisters, coffee cans, coffee can lids, lids to jars, the jars themselves, plastic containers, Pyrex containers, medium to small frying pans—what is in here that couldn't work as a Dresden appliqué circle? Remember, it doesn't need to be perfectly matched to our suggested size to be perfect for your project!

TRACEABLE TEMPLATES

What if you have a fully stocked sewing room and kitchen, but don't have a circle you want to trace? Don't worry! We've got you covered! In the templates and references section of this book, each project that calls for a circle has one you can trace. We've printed several circles for you to use starting on page 208. You can trace ours and cut them out (on template plastic, cereal boxes, soda boxes etc.) to trace and use for appliqué centers.

SURROUNDED WITH INSPIRATION

There's also more than one way to add a circle to the center of a Dresden Plate. Fussy cut fun fabrics and piece them into unique, beautiful circles of your own design. Because you're often using fusible adhesives to hold everything down, you can also use fun stitches along the edges to add a beautiful decorative flourish to your appliqué circle. (You can learn more about this on page 88 in *All About Dresden Applique*.)

Show us your circles on your Dresden projects and share what circles you used as templates as well! You never know, your choice for creating a circle may be super unique, and exactly what inspiration someone else needs to finish off their project perfectly! Put your own spin on finding a center circle for your project—it's going to be sew very beautiful!

DRESDEN BOTANICA

Dresden plates make for the perfect quilt block. With this project, you can create a veritable bed of Dresden flowers fit for any garden. Try this traditional block in all your favorite colors and make your garden grow!

materials

QUILT SIZE
65" x 78½"

- 6 packages of 5" squares
- 3 yards of background fabric
- 1¼ yards of border fabric
- ¾ yards of binding fabric

- 5 yards of backing - vertical seam(s) or 2½ yards of backing 108" wide
- Missouri Star Large Dresden Plate Template for 10" Squares (template on page 211)

Dresden Botanica

STEP 1: CUT

Refer to *Put Your Own Spin On It* on page 22 to find the perfect 3¾- 4″ circle for your project. For this project, you will want a circle that is ½″ larger than your finished center circle. Use the object to trace a circle onto a piece of stiff paper. Cut out the circle to use as your template.

From the 5″ squares:

- Select 20 squares for the center circles.
  - Use your circle template to trace a circle on the reverse side of your selected squares.

  - Cut out each circle.

  - Set your paper template aside for the moment.

- From the remaining squares, align the 5″ mark on the Dresden template with the top of a 5″ square. Cut 1 blade then flip the template 180° and cut a second blade. Each 5″ square will yield 2 blades and a **total of 400** blades are needed. **1A**

From the background fabric, cut (7) 14″ strips across the width of the fabric. Subcut the strips into 14″ squares for a **total of 20** squares.

STEP 2: SEW

Fold 1 blade in half lengthwise with right sides facing. Stitch straight across the larger end. **2A**

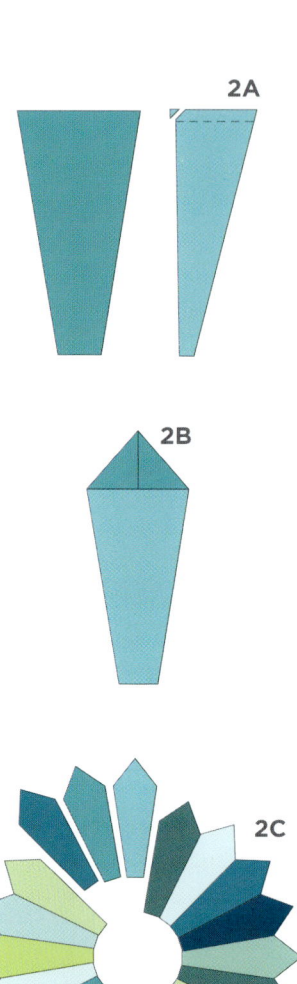

Trim the corner, open the seam, and gently poke out the point. Press—centering the seam. **Make 400. 2B**

Sew 20 blades together to make a Dresden Plate. Sew from the top of the blades to the bottom, backstitching at the top. Press. **2C**

Lightly press 1 background 14″ square in half both directions to create placement lines. Using the creases as a guide, center a Dresden Plate on a square. Pin in place. **2D**

Take the paper circle template and trim ¼″ inside the outer rim of the circle.

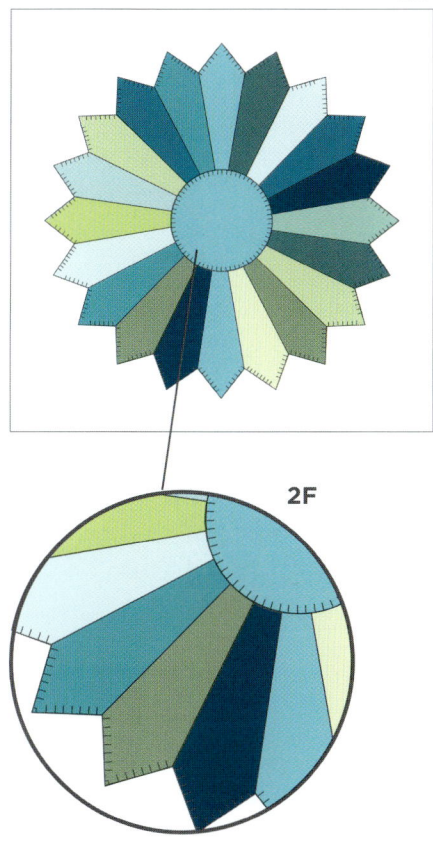

Make a gathering stitch around 1 print circle about ⅛″ in from the edge. Place the paper circle template on the wrong side of the print circle and pull the thread to gather. Press the circle and remove the template.

Center the prepared circle on the Dresden plate and pin in place. Appliqué the plate and the circle to the background square using a zigzag or blanket stitch. **Make 20.** 2E 2F

Block Size: 14″ unfinished, 13½″ finished

STEP 3: ARRANGE & SEW

Arrange the blocks into **5 rows of 6** as shown in diagram **3A**. Sew the blocks together to form rows and press in opposite directions. Nest the seams and sew the rows together. Press.

STEP 4: BORDER

Cut (7) 6″ strips across the width of the fabric. Sew the strips together to make a long strip. Trim the borders from this strip. Measure, cut, and attach the borders to the quilt top. The lengths are approximately 68″ for the sides and 65½″ for the top and bottom. **4A**

STEP 5: QUILT & BIND

Refer to the finishing sections of *How to Create a Quilt* on pages 14-17 to quilt, square and trim, then add binding to finish your quilt.

4A

1. Cut 2 wedges using the Dresden template from each 5" square.

2. Fold the wedge in half vertically and sew across the top of the widest end.

3. Trim the corner, open the seam and turn the point right side out. Press, centering the seam.

4. Sew 20 wedges together.

5. Center the plate on a background square and pin in place.

6. Appliqué the block and the center circle to the background square to complete the block.

33

mini sunflower pillow

Go mini with Dresdens and make a sweet floral pillow. With the right circle selection, you can make a variety of beautiful flower designs. A larger circle turns these into mini sunflowers. Many possibilities, one simple design—it couldn't be easier!

materials

PROJECT SIZE
25" x 25"

- 1 package of 5" print sqares
- ¼ yard of complimentary fabric
- 1½ yards of background fabric
- (1) 27½" square of batting
- ½ yard of border fabric
- ¾ yard of backing
- Missouri Star Large Dresden Plate Template for 10" Squares (template on page 211)
- ½ yard Missouri Star Sew Light fusible adhesive
- Polyester fiberfill

Mini Sunflower Pillow

STEP 1: CUT

Select (14) 5" print squares and set the remaining squares aside for another project.

Cut each selected print square in half to create (2) 2½" x 5" rectangles. Subcut blades from each rectangle by placing the small end of the template on 1 of the long edges of the rectangle and rotating 180° alternatively between cuts. Up to 3 blades can be cut from each rectangle, and a **total of 80** are needed. **1A**

From the complimentary fabric, cut (1) 4½" strip across the width of the fabric. Subcut (4) 4½" squares. Set the remaining fabric aside for another project.

From the background fabric cut:
- (1) 25½" strip across the width of the fabric.
  - Subcut (1) 25½" square.
  - Trim the remainder of the strip into (2) 10" strips and cut (1) 10" square from each strip.

- (1) 27½" strip across the width of the fabric.
  - Subcut (1) 27½" square.
  - Trim the remainder of the strip into (2) 10" strips across the width of the fabric and cut (1) 10" square from each strip. **For a total of (4)** 10" squares.

- Set the remaining fabric aside for another project.

From the backing fabric, cut (1) 25½" strip across the width. Subcut (1) 25½" square.

From the fusible web, cut (1) 4" strip across the width of the fusible web. Cut (4) 4" squares.

STEP 2: MAKE BLADES

Fold 1 Dresden blade in half lengthwise, right sides facing. Sew across the wide end of the folded blade. Trim the folded corner to reduce the bulk and turn the blade right side out. Poke the corner out and press with the seam in the center. Repeat the instructions to fold, sew, trim, turn, and press each blade. **Make 80**. **2A 2B**

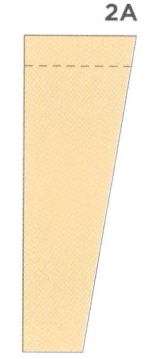

2A

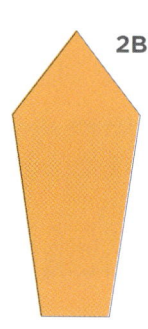

2B

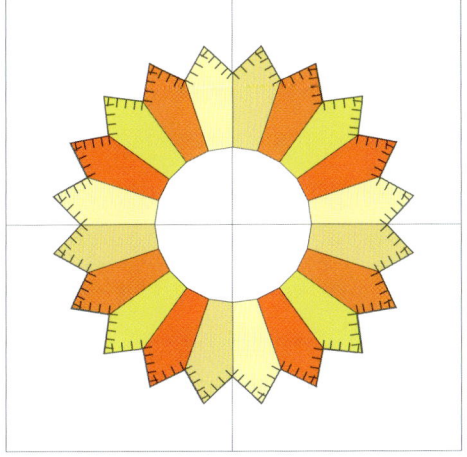

STEP 3: BLOCK CONSTRUCTION

Sew 5 blades together as shown to form a quadrant, alternating colors as you go. Press. **Make 4** quadrants. **3A**

Sew the quadrants together to complete the Dresden circle. Press. **Make 4** Dresden circles. **3B**

Fold (1) 10" background square in half both ways and crease to mark the center. Lay 1 Dresden circle on top of the square and align the seams with the center creases. Pin as needed. Using a blanket or zigzag stitch, appliqué the Dresden circle in place around the outer edge. **3C**

STEP 3: BLOCK CONSTRUCTION (CONTINUED)

Refer to *Put Your Own Spin On It* on page 22 to find the perfect 3¾-4" circle for your project. Use the object to trace a circle onto onto the paper side of a 4" fusible web square. Following the manufacturer's instructions, adhere the fusible web square to the wrong side of a 4½" complimentary square set aside earlier. Cut on the traced line and then remove the paper backing from the circle and discard it.

Fold the fused circle in half both ways and crease to mark the center. Lay the fused circle atop the appliquéd Dresden circle, adhesive side down, and line up the center creases with the seams of the Dresden. When you are happy with your placement, adhere the circle to the Dresden according to the manufacturer's instructions. Using a blanket or zigzag stitch, appliqué the circle in place. Repeat the process to appliqué the remaining Dresdens and center circles to the 10" background squares. **Make 4** Mini Sunflower blocks. **3D**

Block Size: 10" unfinished, 9½" finished

3D

4A

STEP 4: ARRANGE & SEW

Refer to diagram to lay out your blocks in 2 rows of 2. Sew the blocks together in rows. Press the seams in opposite directions. Nest the seams and sew the rows together to complete the pillow center. **4A**

STEP 5: BORDER

Cut (3) 3½" strips across the width of the fabric. Sew them together to make a long strip. Measure, cut, and attach the borders to the project top The approximate lengths are 19½" for the sides and 25½" for the top and bottom.

STEP 6: QUILT

Layer the project with batting and backing, then quilt. Trim the batting and backing even with the edges of your quilted pillow top.

STEP 7: MAKE THE PILLOW

Place the pillow top and the 25½" square together, right sides facing. With pins, mark a 6" opening on 1 of the sides. Start by backstitching at a pin, sew around the pillow until you reach the next pin, then backstitch again. Clip the corners. **7A**

Clip the corners. Turn right side out and gently push the corners out. Press. At the opening, turn the seam allowance to the inside and hold it taut as you press. This will give you a sewing line to use when you hand stitch the opening closed. Stuff with fiberfill.. Close the opening using an invisible hand stitch.

5A

7A

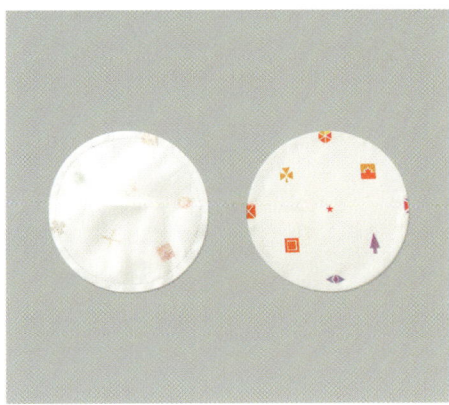

1. Subcut blades from each rectangle by placing the small end of the template on 1 of the long edges of the rectangle and rotating 180° alternatively between Cuts. A total of 80 are needed.

2. Fold 1 Dresden blade in half lengthwise, right sides together. Sew across the wide end of the folded blade. Trim the folded corner to reduce the bulk and turn the blade right side out. Poke the corner out and press. Make 80.

3. Lay the marked interfacing square atop a background print square. Sew on the marked circle. Trim and turn right sides out. Do not press. Make 4.

4. Sew 20 Dresden blades together to complete a Dresden plate. Backstitch at the outside end of each seam. Make 4.

GRANDMOTHER'S FAN

Elegant and simple, this project is so much easier than it looks! By sewing a few Dresdens together into a quarter-circle, you can create a beautiful, traditional fan shape. We arranged our grandmother's fans into a sweet stripe across the quilt and just love this look!

materials

QUILT SIZE
65" x 78½"

- 3 packages of 5" print squares
- 1 package of 10" background squares
- 1½ yard of border fabric
   - includes fabric for quarter circles
- ¾ yard of binding fabric
- 4¾ yards of backing - vertical seam(s) or 2½ yards of backing 108" wide
- Missouri Star Large Dresden Plate Template for 10" Squares (template on page 211)

Grandmother's Fan

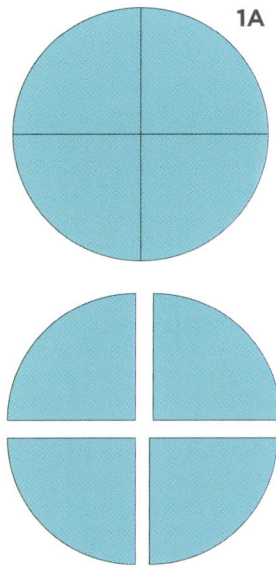

STEP 1: CUT

From the border fabric, cut:
- (2) 5" strips across the width of the fabric. Subcut a **total of (11)** 5" squares.
  - Refer to *Put Your Own Spin On It* on page 22 to find the perfect 4¾-5" circle for your project. Use the object to trace a circle onto each of the 5" squares. Fold each circle in half twice, once vertically and horizontally. Cut along the fold lines to make quarter circles. **1A**

- Set the remaining fabric aside for the border.

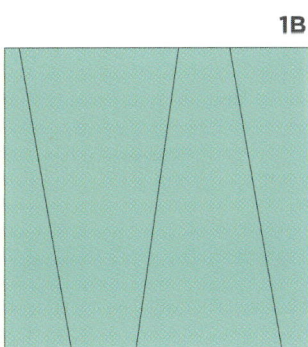

From the 5" print squares, cut a **total of 210** blades. Align the 5" mark on the template with the top of the square. Cut 1 blade then flip the template 180° and cut a second blade. Each square will yield 2 blades. **1B**

Set the remaining squares aside for another project.

STEP 2: SEW

Sew 5 blades together to make a fan.
Make 42. 2A

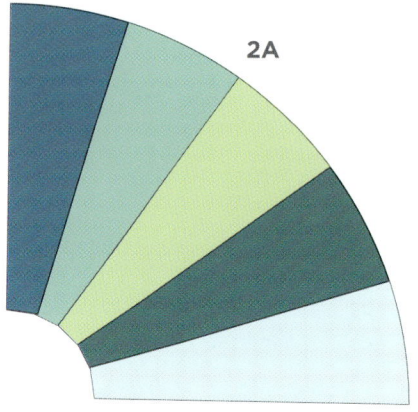

STEP 3: APPLIQUÉ

Using a small blanket stitch or zigzag, appliqué a fan to 1 corner of a 10″ background square. Place a quarter circle on the corner, covering up the raw ends of the blades. Appliqué in place to complete the block. Repeat to **make 42** blocks. **3A**

Block Size: 10″ unfinished, 9½″ finished

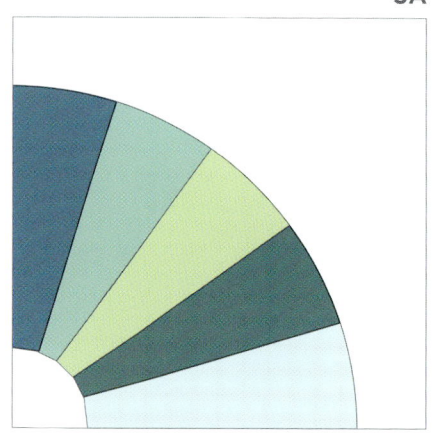

4A

STEP 4: ARRANGE & SEW

Follow diagram **4A** to lay out the blocks in **7 rows of 6**. Notice how the blocks are oriented. Sew the blocks into rows and press the rows in opposite directions. Nest the seams and sew the rows together. Press.

STEP 5: BORDER

Cut (7) 5" strips across the width of the fabric. Sew the strips together to make a long strip. Measure, cut, and attach the borders to the quilt top. The lengths are approximately 67" for the sides and 66½" for the top and bottom. **5A**

STEP 6: QUILT & BIND

Refer to the finishing sections of *How to Create a Quilt* on pages 14-17 to quilt, square and trim, then add binding to finish your project.

5A

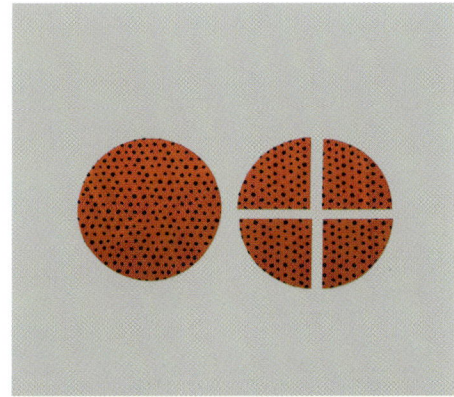

1. Cut each 4¾-5″ circle in half vertically and horizontally to create 4 quarter-circles.

2. Align the 5″ mark on the Dresden template with the top of a 5″ square. Cut 1 blade, then flip the template 180° and cut a second blade.

3. Sew 5 blades together to make a fan.

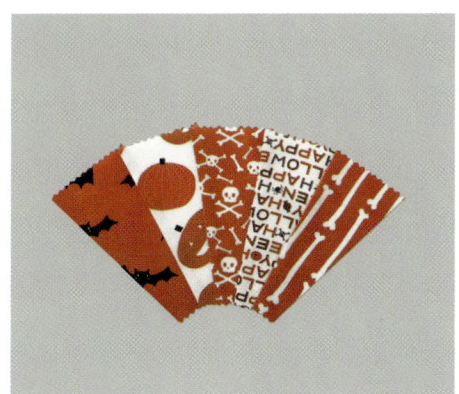

4. Using a small blanket stitch or a zigzag, appliqué a fan to one corner of a 10″ background square.

5. Place a quarter circle on the corner, covering up the raw ends of the blades. Appliqué in place to complete the block.

HERE COMES THE SUN

The sun doesn't just rise in the east anymore! Now you can create a whole quilt full of wonderful little sunrises with this fun and simple project. Simply sew the Dresdens into a half circle, and watch all the suns come up! Holding the power of the sun in your hands has never been so easy!

materials

QUILT SIZE
81" x 94½"

- 1 package of 10" print squares
- 5½ yards of background fabric
- ½ yard of complementary fabric
- ¾ yard of binding fabric
- 7½ yards of backing - horizontal seam(s) or 2½ yards of 108" wide backing
- 2 yards of Heat n Bond - Feather Weight Fusible Interfacing
- ¼ yard of fusible interfacing
- Missouri Star Large Dresden Plate Template for 10" Squares (template on page 211)

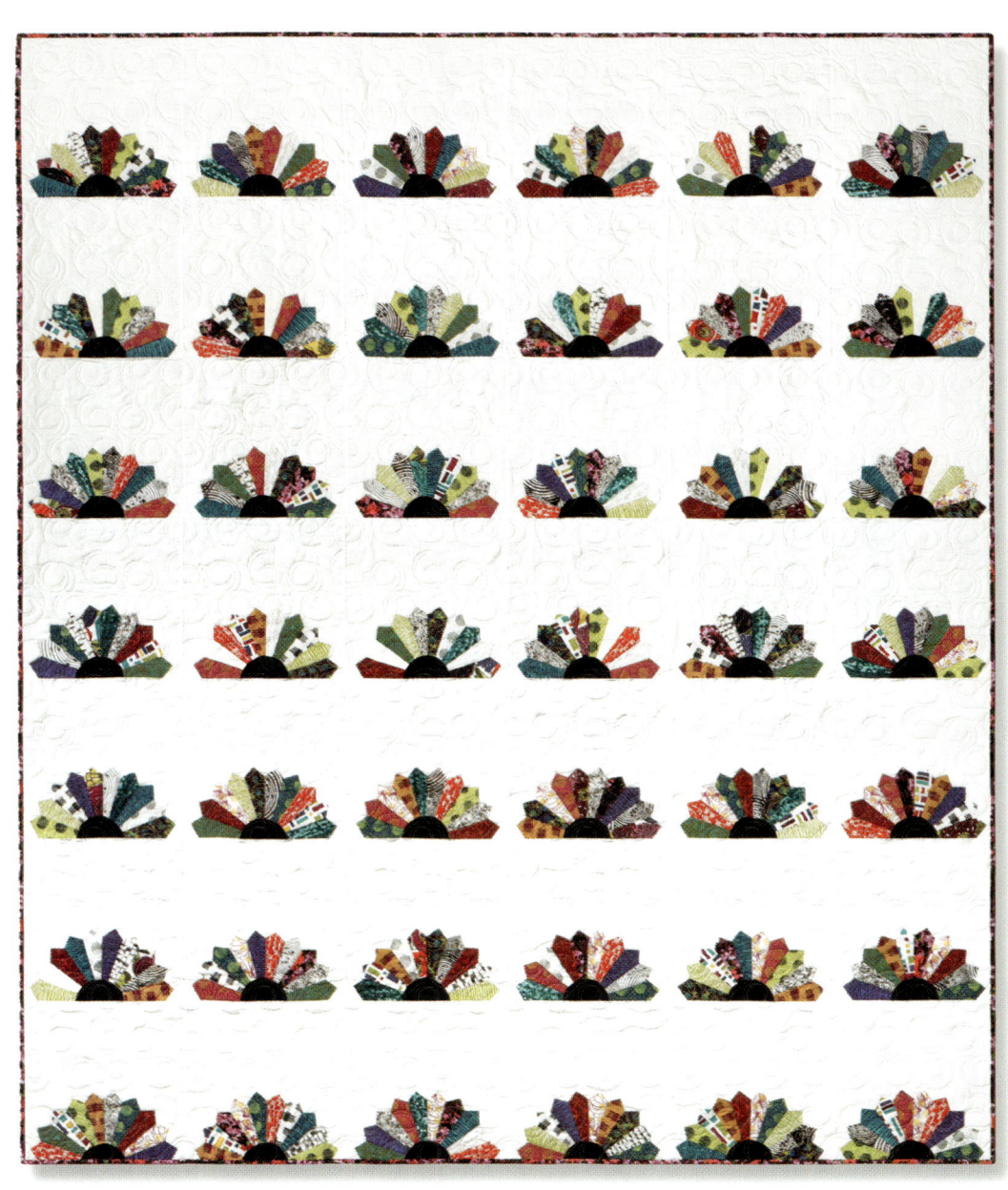

Here Comes The Sun

STEP 1: CUT

From the 10" print squares, cut each square in half to create (2) 5" x 10" rectangles. Use the template to subcut each rectangle into 5" Dresden blades. Each rectangle will yield 5 blades and a **total of 420** are needed. **1A**

From the background fabric, cut (14) 14" strips across the width of the fabric, subcut the strips into 14" squares for a **total of 42** squares.

From the complementary fabric, cut:
- (3) 5" wide strips across the width of the fabric—Subcut the strips into 5" squares for a **total of 21** squares.

From the fusible, cut (6) 5" wide strips across the width of the fabric, subcut the strips into 5" squares for a **total of 21** squares.

1A

STEP 2: SEW

Fold 1 blade in half lengthwise, with right sides facing. Stitch straight across the larger end. **2A**

Trim the corner, open the seam and turn the point right side out. Press, centering the seam. **Make 420** blades. **2B**

Join 10 blades to make a half-Dresden fan. Begin sewing at the top of the blade and stop at the bottom. Be sure to backstitch at the top of the blade. Press all seams to 1 side. **2C**

Lightly press 1 background 14″ square in half vertically to make a placement line. Using the crease as a guide, center a Dresden fan on a square with the bottom edge of the fan aligned with the edge of the background square. Pin in place. **2D**

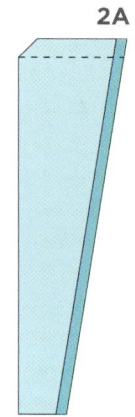

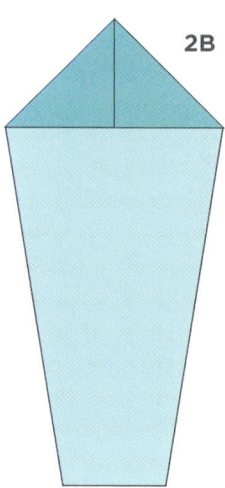

2C

2D

Refer to *Put Your Own Spin On It* on page 22 to find the perfect size of circle for your project. Use the object to trace a 4 - 4½" circle onto the non-adhesive side of 21 fusible squares and 21 squares of complementary fabric. Cut each fusible and complementary fabric square along your drawn line to **make 21** circles of each. Lay 1 fusible circle atop a fabric circle—adhesive (bumpy) side facing the right side of the fabric. Sew all the way around the circles using a ¼" seam allowance. Cut the circle in half to **make 42** half-circles and turn right side out. Smooth the curved edge. *Do not press!*

Center the prepared half-circle on the Dresden fan. Follow the manufacturer's instructions to adhere your half-circle in place.

Appliqué the Dresden fan and the half-circle to the background square using a small zigzag or blanket stitch to complete the block. **Make 42. 2E**

Block Size: 14" unfinished, 13½" finished

2E

STEP 3: ARRANGE & SEW

Arrange the blocks into **7 rows of 6** as shown in diagram **3A** on the right. When you are happy with the arrangement, sew the blocks together to form rows. Press the seams of each row in opposite directions. Nest the seams and sew the rows together. Press.

STEP 4: QUILT & BIND

Refer to the finishing sections of *How to Create a Quilt* on pages 14-17 to quilt, square and trim, then add binding to finish your quilt.

3A

1. Fold a wedge in half lengthwise with right sides facing. Stitch straight across the larger end.

2. Trim the corner at an angle, open the seam, and turn the point right side out. Press.

3. Join 10 blades to make a half-Dresden Plate.

4. Lightly press a background 14" square in half vertically to make a placement line. Using the crease as a guide, center a half-Dresden Plate on the square with the bottom edge aligned with the edge of the background square. Pin in place.

5. Trace the outside edge of the circle template onto the non-adhesive side of a fusible square and a complementary square. Cut each along the drawn line. Layer the two circles together with right sides facing and sew them together using a ¼" seam allowance.

6. After cutting the circle in half and turning it right side out, center the half-circle on the half-Dresden Plate. Fuse in place and stitch around the half-circle using a small zigzag or buttonhole stitch.

FANCY DRESDEN FANS

Create a mosaic of Dresden Plates with these fancy fans. Making full, half and three-quarter plates, some easy piecing, and brave trimming builds a beautiful quilt from the center out. Be fancy free, it's as easy as can be!

materials

QUILT SIZE
75" x 75"

- 3 packages of 5" print squares
- 3¼ yards of background fabric
- ¾ of a yard of inner border fabric
- 1½ yards of outer border fabric

- 5 yards (vertical seams) or 2½ yards of 108" wide backing
- Missouri Star Large Dresden Plate Template for 10" Squares (template on page 211)
- ¾ of a yard of fusible interfacing (20" wide)

THIS QUILT IS PART OF A MISSOURI STAR TRIPLE PLAY!

Open Camera, Scan Code, Watch Misty make her Fancy Dresden Fans quilt!

Fancy Dresden Fans

STEP 1: CUT

From each 5" print square, cut 2 Dresden blades using the template. You'll need to rotate the template 180° to get 2 blades from each square.

From the outer border fabric, cut (8) 6" strips across the width of the fabric. Cut (1) 6" x 17" rectangle from 1 of the strips and set the rest of the strip and the other 7 strips aside for the outer border. Trim the 6" x 17" rectangle to 5" x 17" then subcut 8 blades from the rectangle. Add these to those previously cut for a **total of 260**.

From the background fabric, cut (13) 8" strips and (2) 4" strips across the width of the fabric. Subcut each 8" strip into (5) 8" squares for a **total of (64)** 8" squares. Subcut the 4" strips into 4" squares. Each strip will yield up to 10 squares and a **total of (21)** 4" squares.

From the fusible interfacing, cut (5) 4" strips across the width of the interfacing. Subcut a **total of (21)** 4" squares.

STEP 2: MAKE THE BLADES

Fold a Dresden blade in half lengthwise, right sides facing. Sew across the wide end of the folded blade. **2A**

Clip the corner and turn the blade right side out. Poke the corner out and press with the seam in the center. Repeat to **make 260** blades. **2B**

STEP 3: MAKE THE FANS & PLATES

Select 10 blades and sew them together along the long sides to form a 10 blade fan.* Press. Fold the long edge of each end blade under ¼" and press. **Make 12**. **3A**

Select 15 blades and sew them together* as before to form a 15 blade fan. Fold the long edge of each end blade under ¼" and press. **Make 8**. **3B**

Select 20 blades and sew them together* as before to form a Dresden plate. Backstitch at the outside edge of each seam. Press. **3C**

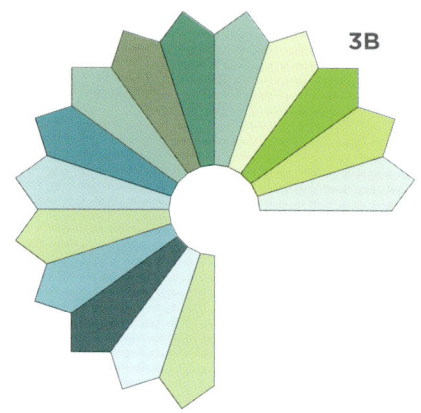

***Note**: Backstitch at the outside edge of each seam.

STEP 4: MAKE THE CENTER CIRCLES

Refer to *Put Your Own Spin On It* on page 22 to find the perfect 3¼- 3¾" circle for your project. Use the object to trace a circle onto on the non-adhesive side of each 4" fusible interfacing square. Cut a slit in the center of the drawn circle. Lay the marked interfacing square atop a 4" background square with the glue side of the interfacing touching the right side of the background square. **4A**

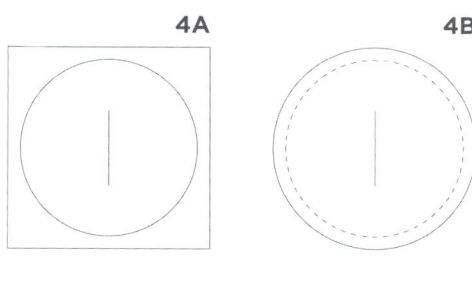

Sew the pieces together by stitching on the marked circle. Trim ¼" away from the sewn line. **4B**

Turn the sewn circle right sides out through the slit and push out the edges. Do not press. **Make 21** center circles. **4C**

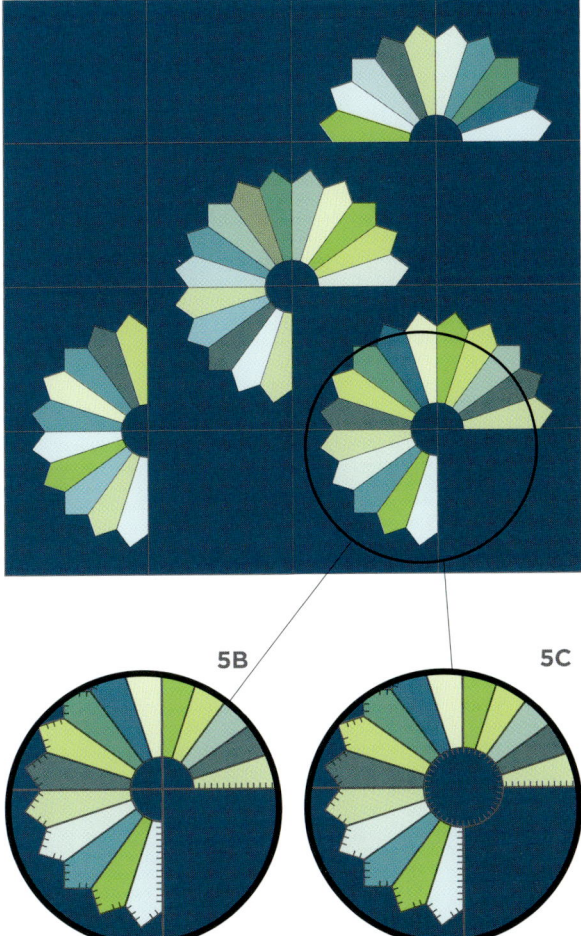

STEP 5: MAKE QUADRANTS

Pick up (16) 8" background squares and sew them together in **4 rows of 4**. Press the seams of each row in opposite directions. Nest the seams and sew the rows together. Press.

Pick up (2) 10 blade fans and (2) 15 blade fans and arrange them on the background quadrant as shown. Use the seams of the background quadrant as a guide to place the fans on the background quadrant. Pin in place as necessary. **5A**

Use a small blanket or zigzag stitch around the perimeter of each Dresden fan to appliqué each fan in place. **5B**

Fold each center circle in half twice to mark the center. Place a center circle at the void left in each Dresden fan. Fuse in place and then use a small blanket or zigzag stitch around the perimeter of each circle to appliqué in place. **5C**

Make 4 quadrants.

STEP 6: ARRANGE & SEW

Arrange the quadrants as shown. Note the orientation of each quadrant. Sew the quadrants together to form the quilt center. Press. **6A**

Repeat the steps in section 5 to attach the remaining Dresden fans, Dresden plate, and center circles to the quilt top. **Note**: Each of the remaining Dresden fans and plates will cross the seams you just made sewing the quadrants together.

STEP 7: INNER BORDER

Refer to diagram **7A** for border placement. Cut (7) 2½" strips across the width of the inner border fabric. Sew the strips together to make 1 long strip. Trim the inner borders from this strip. Measure, cut, and attach the inner borders to the quilt top. The approximate lengths are 60½" for the sides and 64½" for the top and bottom.

STEP 8: OUTER BORDER

Pick up the 6" strips you set aside earlier and sew them together to make 1 long strip. Trim the outer borders from this strip. Measure, cut, and attach the outer borders to the quilt top. The approximate lengths are 64½" for the sides and 75½" for the top and bottom.

STEP 9: QUILT & BIND

Refer to the finishing sections of *How to Create a Quilt* on pages 14-17 to quilt, square and trim, then add binding to finish your quilt.

7A

1. Fold a Dresden blade in half lengthwise, right sides facing. Sew across the wide end of the folded blade. Clip the corner and turn the blade right side out. Poke the corner out and press with the seam in the center. Make 260 blades.

2. Select 10 blades and sew them together along the long sides. Press. Turn the 2 unfinished edges under ¼" and press. Make 12.

3. Select 15 blades and sew them together along the long sides. Press. Turn the 2 unfinished edges under ¼" and press. Make 8.

4. Select 20 blades and sew them together along the long sides. Press.

5. Trace a circle on a fusible interfacing square. Cut a slit in the center. Lay the traced circle atop a 4" background square with the glue side touching the right side of the fabric. Sew on the traced line and then turn the circle right side out.

6. Attach the Dresden fans and plates to the squares as instructed in the pattern. To add a center circle, fold to mark the center and then line up the folds with the blades. Fuse in place then appliqué around the outer edge.

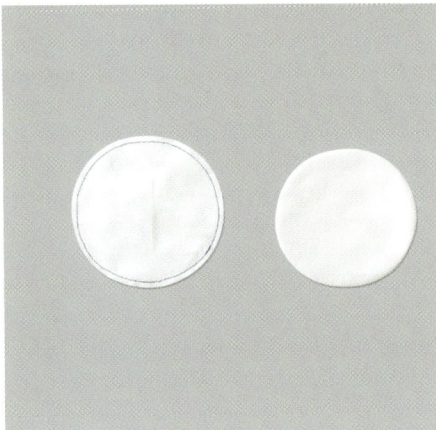

TINY DRESDENS

This Dresden plate quilt starts with teensy weensy Dresden petals, followed quickly by big and bold center circles. The way these look put us in mind of Sunflowers blooming along an old country road in the summer sun. You can have your own garden of sunflowers that you created yourself, by just following this very simple pattern.

materials

QUILT SIZE
81" x 94½"

- 1 roll of 2½" print strips
- 4 packages of 5" background squares
- ½ yard of border fabric
- ½ yard of binding fabric
- 3¾ yard of backing- horizontal seam(s)
- Missouri Star Large Dresden Plate Template for 10" Squares (template on page 211)
- 1¼ yards of fusible interfacing (20" wide)
- Bamboo pressing stick - optional

THIS QUILT IS PART OF A MISSOURI STAR TRIPLE PLAY!

Open Camera, Scan Code, Watch Jenny make her Tiny Dresdens quilt!

Tiny Dresdens

STEP 1: CUT

Select (22) 2½" print strips from your roll and keep them folded in half. Lay the narrow end of the template on the edge of the strip to cut Dresden blades from the folded strips. Rotate the template 180° after each Dresden blade is cut. Each strip will yield at least 28 Dresden blades and a **total of 600** are needed. **1A**

Set the remainng 2½" print strips aside for another project.

Cut (8) 5" strips across with width of the interfacing. Subcut 5" squares from the strips. Each strip will yield 4 squares and a **total of 30** are needed.

STEP 2: MAKE 4-PATCHES

Select (120) 5" background print squares and set the remaining squares aside for the moment.

Choose 4 different background print squares and arrange them in a 4-patch formation. Sew the squares together in 2 rows. Press the rows in opposite directions. Nest the seams and sew the rows together. Press. **Make (30)** 4-patches. **2A**

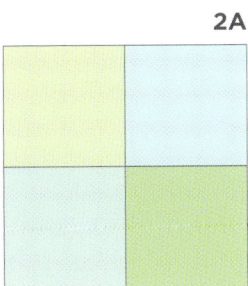

STEP 3: MAKE THE DRESDEN BLADES

Fold 1 Dresden blade in half lengthwise, right sides facing. Sew across the wide end of the folded blade. Trim the folded corner to reduce the bulk and turn the blade right side out. Poke the corner out and press with the seam in the center. Repeat the instructions to fold, sew, trim, turn, and press each blade. **Make 600** blades. **3A 3B**

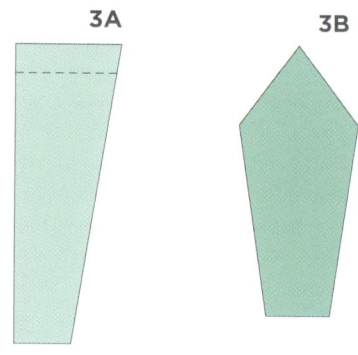

STEP 4: MAKE THE CENTER CIRCLES

Pick up the 5" fusible interfacing squares. Refer to *Put Your Own Spin On It* on page 22 to find the perfect 4-4½" circle for your project. Use the object to trace a circle onto non-adhesive side of (1) 5" square of fusible interfacing. Cut a 2" slit in the center of the drawn circle. Lay the marked interfacing square atop a background print square with the adhesive side of the interfacing touching the right side of the background print square. **4A**

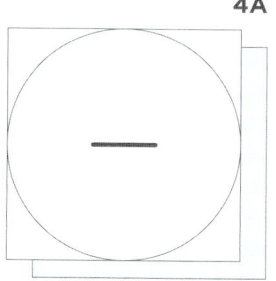

Sew the pieces together by stitching on the marked circle. Trim ¼" away from the sewn line. **4B**

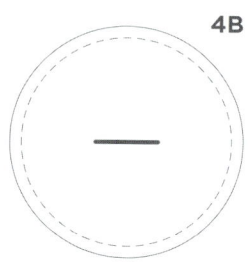

Turn the sewn circle right sides out through the slit and push out the edges with a bamboo stick. Do not press. **Make 30** center circles. **4C**

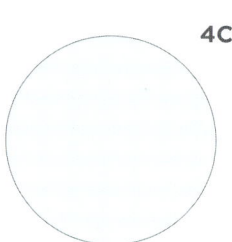

5A

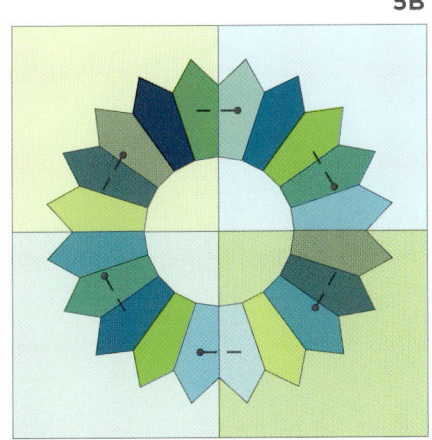
5B

5C

STEP 5: BLOCK CONSTRUCTION

Sew 20 Dresden blades together to complete a Dresden plate. Backstitch at the outside end of each seam. Press. **Make 30** Dresden plates. **5A**

Lay a Dresden plate on top of a 4-patch and align the center seams. Pin as needed around the outside edge. **5B**

Select 1 center circle and fold it in half twice to crease the center mark. Lay the center circle atop the Dresden plate, adhesive side down, and line up the center creases with the seams of the Dresden plate. Adhere the center circle to the Dresden plate according to the manufacturer's instructions. Using a blanket or zigzag stitch, appliqué the center circle and Dresden plate in place. Repeat to **make 30** blocks. **5C**

Block Size: 9½" unfinished, 9" finished

STEP 6: ARRANGE & SEW

Refer to diagram **6A** to the right to lay out your blocks in **6 rows** of **5 blocks**. Sew the blocks together in rows. Press the rows in opposite directions. Nest the seams and sew the rows together. Press.

STEP 7: BORDER

Cut (5) 2½" strips across the width of the border fabric. Sew the strips together end-to-end to make 1 long strip. Trim the borders from this strip. Measure, cut, and attach the borders to the quilt top. The approximate lengths are 54½" for the sides and 49½" for the top and bottom.

STEP 8: QUILT & BIND

Layer the quilt with batting and backing then quilt. After the quilting is complete, refer to the finishing sections of *How to Create a Quilt* on pages 14-17 to quilt, square and trim, then add binding to finish your quilt.

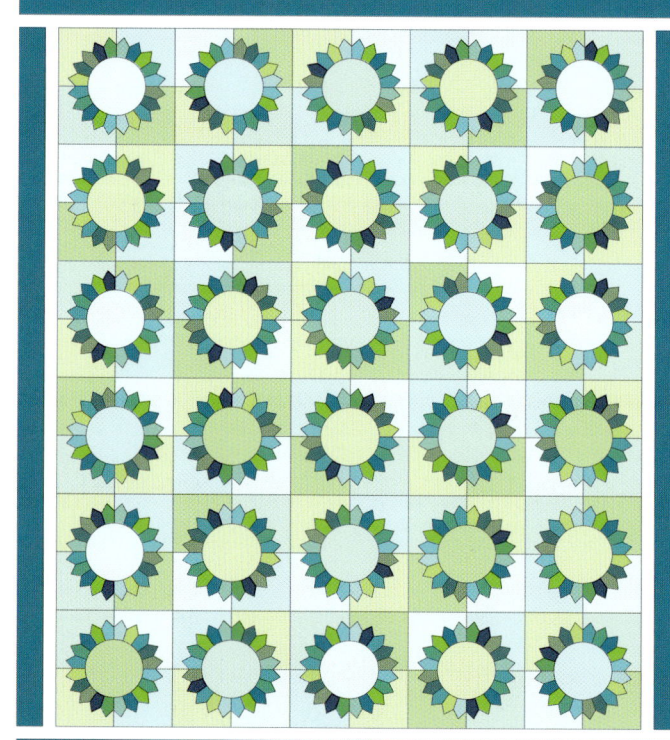

6A

1. Use the mini Dresden template to cut Dresden blades from the folded strips. Each strip will yield at least 28 Dresden blades and a total of 600 are needed.

2. Select 4 different background print squares and arrange them in a 4-patch formation. Sew the squares together in 2 rows and press in opposite directions. Nest the seams and sew the rows together. Press. Make 30.

3. Fold 1 Dresden blade in half lengthwise, right sides together. Sew across the wide end of the folded blade. Trim the folded corner to reduce the bulk and turn the blade right side out. Poke the corner out and press. Make 600.

4. Lay the marked interfacing square atop a background print square. Sew on the marked circle. Trim and turn right sides out. Do not press. Make 30.

5. Sew 20 Dresden blades together to complete a Dresden plate. Backstitch at the outside end of each seam. Make 30.

6. Lay a Dresden plate on top of a 4-patch and align the center seams. Pin. Fold 1 center circle in half twice and crease. Lay the circle atop the Dresden plate, adhesive side down, and line up the center creases. Adhere. Appliqué in place. Make 30.

TURKEY TROT

Just in time for Turkey Day, these adorable little gobblers will cheer you on a Thanksgiving themed quilt. Dresdens create the fan that gives these cute little guys their extravagant tails. With their teensy, weensy little legs and beaks, you'll just want to gobble them up!

materials

QULT SIZE
58½" x 68"

- 2 packages of 5" print squares
- ½ yard of accent fabric
- 2¼ yards of background fabric
- 1¼ yards of border fabric
- ¾ yard of binding
- 3¾ yards of backing fabric horizontal seam(s)
- Missouri Star Large Dresden Plate Template for 10" Squares (template on page 211)
- 1¼ yards of Heat n Bond Lite

Turkey Trot

1A

STEP 1: SORT & CUT

From the 5" print squares:
- Set 5 squares aside for the turkey heads.

- Set 7 squares aside for the legs and beaks.

- Set 15 squares aside for the turkey bodies.

- Cut 35 squares in half, creating 2½" x 5" rectangles. Use the Mini Dresden template to cut 3 Dresden shapes from each rectangle for a **total of 210**. **1A**

- Trim 15 squares to 4" for Irish Change centers.

- Set the remaining 5" squares aside for another project.

From the accent fabric, cut (6) 2" strips across the width of the fabric. Cut 2 strips in half to create 4 short strips.

STEP 1: SORT & CUT (CONTINUED)

From the background fabric, cut:
- (4) 10" strips across the width of the fabric. Subcut a **total of (15)** 10" squares.

- (2) 7" strips across the width of the fabric. Cut 1 strip in half to create 2 short strips. Set 1 short strip aside for section 3 and from the other short strip, cut (2) 2" strips across the width of the strip. Subcut (3) 2" x 7" rectangles from each 2" strip.

- (2) 4" strips across the width of the fabric. Cut 1 strip in half to create 2 short strips. From 1 short strip, cut (2) 2" strips across the width of the strip.

- (8) 2" strips across the width of the fabric. Subcut 4 strips into 2" x 7" rectangles. Add these to the rectangles previously cut for a **total of 30**.

From the Heat n Bond, cut (9) 4¾" strips across the width of the fusible. Subcut a **total of (27)** 4¾" squares.

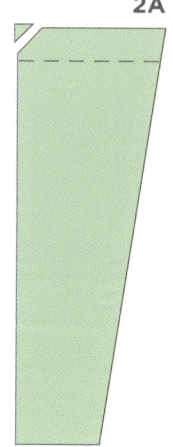

2A

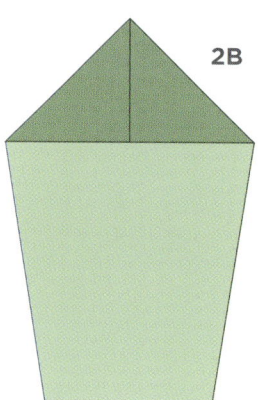

2B

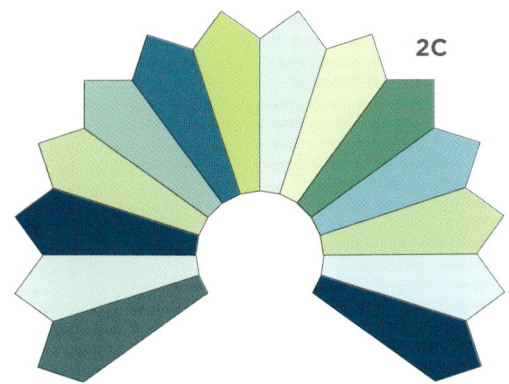

STEP 2: MAKE THE TURKEY BLOCKS

Sew Feathers
Fold each mini Dresden in half lengthwise, right sides facing. Stitch straight across the larger end using a ¼" seam allowance. Trim the folded corner as shown, open the seam, and turn the point right side out. Press, centering the seam.
Make 210 feathers. **2A 2B**

Join 14 feathers to make a turkey tail. Begin sewing at the top of the feather and stop at the bottom. Be sure to backstitch at the top of the feather and press all seams to 1 side. **Make 15**. **2C**

Crease each 10" background square in half vertically. Using the creases as a guide, center a turkey tail horizontally on the background square about 1¾" down from the top. Pin in place. Appliqué the turkey tail to the background square using a blanket or small zigzag stitch. **Make 15**. **2D**

STEP 2: MAKE THE TURKEY BLOCKS (CONTINUED)

Trace & Fuse
Use the turkey templates found on page 209 for the turkey appliqué. Trace 3 turkey heads each onto the paper side of 5 squares of fusible web. Trace 15 *pairs* of legs and 15 beaks* onto the paper side of 7 squares of fusible web. Trace a body onto the paper side of 15 squares of fusible web. Adhere each square to the reverse side of the corresponding 5″ print squares set aside earlier. Cut out the shapes and remove the paper backing. ***Note**: We cut some of our beaks freehand from other scraps of fused squares to add more variety.

Lay a block with feathers attached right side up on your pressing surface. Lay a turkey body on top of the tail feathers, making sure to cover the circular void. Set a turkey head on top, then slide a pair of feet underneath the bottom edge of the turkey head. **Tip**: Not all of your turkey feet have to be straight. We arranged a few of our turkeys' feet at different angles to let them dance! Place a beak on top. Once you're happy with the placement of each piece, follow the manufacturer's instructions to adhere them to your block. **2E**

Appliqué
Stitch around the edges of the fused fabric using a blanket or small zigzag stitch to complete the block. Set aside. **Make 15**. **2F**

Block Size: 10″ unfinished, 9½″ finished

2E

2F

STEP 3: MAKE THE A, B, & C UNITS FOR THE IRISH CHANGE BLOCKS

A units

Chain stitch the 4″ print squares to 2 of the long 2″ background strips. To chain stitch, place the first square near the edge of your background strip, right sides together, then sew it in place. Sew a couple of stitches past the end of the square and leave your needle in the work. Place the next square on top of the strip, then sew it in place. Repeat until you have the 15 squares added to the strips. **3A**

Note: For the next step, you can leave the squares on the long strip or separate them by cutting the strip in between the squares.

Chain stitch the opposite side of the square units to the 2 remaining 2″ background strips. Trim the units even with the edges of the 4″ squares. Press towards the squares for a **total of 15** A units. **3B**

STEP 3: MAKE THE A, B, & C UNITS FOR THE IRISH CHANGE BLOCKS (CONTINUED)

B units

Sew a 2" accent strip to both sides of a 4" background strip. Press the seams toward the accent fabric. **Make 1** full strip set and **make 1** short strip set.

Cut each of these strip sets into 2" increments for a **total of 30** B units. **3C**

C units

Sew a 2" accent strip to both sides of a 7" background strip. Press the seams toward the background fabric. **Make 1** full strip set and **make 1** short strip set.

Cut each of these strip sets into 2" increments for a **total of 30** C units. **3D**

STEP 4: MAKE THE IRISH CHANGE BLOCKS

Lay 1 A unit and 2 B units in 3 rows as shown. Nest the seams and sew the rows together to complete the block center. Press. **4A**

Sew a 2" x 7" background rectangle to both sides of the block center. Press the seams toward the outside edges. **4B**

Sew a C unit to the top and bottom of the center unit, nesting the seams as you go. Repeat the previous instructions to **make 15** blocks. Press. **4C 4D**

Block Size: 10" unfinished, 9½" finished

STEP 5: ARRANGE & SEW

Arrange the blocks into **6 rows of 5** as shown in the diagram **5A** on the right. Notice how the blocks alternate. Sew the blocks together to form rows and press in opposite directions. Nest the seams and sew the rows together. Press.

STEP 6: BORDER

Cut (6) 6" strips across the width of the border fabric. Sew the strips together to make 1 long strip. Trim the borders from this strip. Measure, cut, and attach the borders to the quilt top. The strip lengths are approximately 57½" for the sides and 59" for the top and bottom.

STEP 7: QUILT & BIND

Refer to the finishing sections of *How to Create a Quilt* on pages 14-17 to quilt, square and trim, then add binding to finish your quilt.

5A

1. Fold a Dresden blade in half lengthwise, right sides facing. Sew across the wide end. Clip the corner and turn the blade right side out. Poke the corner out and press. Make 210 Feathers.

2. Join 14 feathers to make a turkey tail. Make 15.

3. Crease a 10″ background square in half vertically. Using the crease as a guide, center a turkey tail horizontally on the background square about 1¾″ down from the top. Pin in place. Appliqué the turkey tail to the background square using a blanket or small zigzag stitch. Make 15.

4. Lay a turkey body on top of the tail feathers, making sure to cover the circular void. Set a turkey head on top, then slide a pair of feet underneath the bottom edge of the turkey head. Once you're happy with the placement of each piece, place a beak on top and fuse them to your block.

5. Stitch around the edges of the fused fabric using a blanket or small zigzag stitch to complete the block. Set aside. Make 15.

ALL ABOUT DRESDEN APPLIQUÉ

Are you ready to have some fun with fabric? Let's talk about appliqué! Appliqué—or applying shaped patches of fabric to a background to form a picture or pattern—opens so many doors of what's possible when it comes to quiltmaking. No longer are you confined to basic shapes that can be achieved through patchwork like squares and triangles. All the Dresden shapes and circles we create are fast and easy thanks to appliqué!

The *Dresden Tree* (pg. 94) project calls for appliqué to add layered elements, building the boughs so you can deck your halls. The *Dresden Botanica* (pg. 26) is another project that combines piecing and appliqué as you stitch down the Dresden Plates and the center circles to cover raw edges. If you are just getting started with appliqué, let me tell you that it is a fun and easy process to learn, and you'll be amazed at what you can create.

There are a few different methods of appliqué, some of which require a sewing machine and others that don't. The method we recommend most often to beginners is called "fusible appliqué", and we finish our edges on the sewing machine. We love using a fusible product to adhere fabric shapes to the quilt because it's fast, easy, and long-lasting through many washes. Ready to try your hand at fusible appliqué? There are a few supplies you'll want to have on hand before you get started.

SUPPLIES

FABRIC & TEMPLATES

Appliqués can be cut from solid or print fabrics, and scraps are perfect for this! The appliqué patterns in this book also include the templates you can trace onto the paper side of a fusible product to make your own fabric shapes. **Tip:** Unless your shapes are all symmetrical, be sure to reverse the images before tracing them onto the fusible web (which adheres to the wrong side of the fabric). It takes a little getting used to, but the first time you cut out a backward fabric shape on accident, you'll learn the lesson quickly! For this book, most shapes are symmetrical and/or circles. You're all set!

FUSIBLE WEB (IRON-ON ADHESIVE)

What exactly is fusible web? In short, it's a thin layer of glue paper that gets pressed to the wrong side of two fabrics to adhere them together. Today's lightweight fusible webs are heat-activated and pressure-sensitive, so they will permanently affix fabrics when you use an iron and follow the manufacturer's instructions. For the appliqué projects in this book, you'll be pleased with a lightweight fusible web like Missouri Star Sew Light Fusible Adhesive.

IRON & TEFLON PRESSING SHEET

An iron is what gives fusible web its magic powers. But make sure not to iron directly on top of fusible products unless you want your iron plate to become a sticky surface. I recommend using a special heat-resistant Teflon sheet to protect your iron from the adhesive that may wish to sneak out the sides of an appliqué patch and attach itself to your iron.

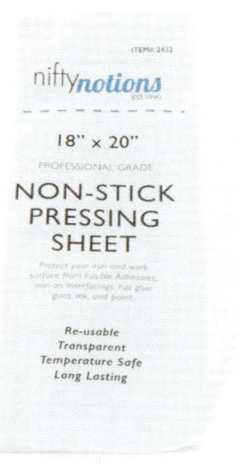

SUPPLIES

SCISSORS

For cutting around tight curves (think fabric letter appliqués), a pair of small, sharp scissors usually does the trick.

OPEN-TOE SEWING MACHINE FOOT

After adhering an appliqué to a quilt block, I like to use my sewing machine's open toe foot so nothing gets in the way of seeing my needle glide around the shape. It's often made of clear plastic so you can see what you're sewing with ease.

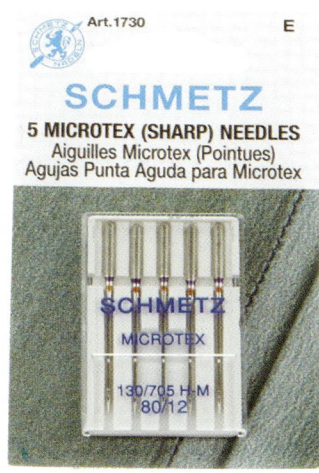

NEEDLE & THREAD

Speaking of needles, a Microtex 80/12 needle is my favorite choice for appliqué. The slim, sharp point pierces through densely woven fabrics with ease. A basic 50 weight cotton thread works well. If you want your thread to blend into the quilt, choose a thread color that matches the appliqué patch. Once you are more comfortable sewing around appliqués, you may want to change up the look of your stitch with a thicker 40 weight thread in a contrasting or variegated color.

WHAT THREAD COLOR SHOULD YOU PICK FOR APPLIQUÉ?

A thread that matches your design is more forgiving for those just starting out. Stitching down multiple colors? Choose a neutral or a bright color you love.

APPLIQUÉ TIPS & TRICKS

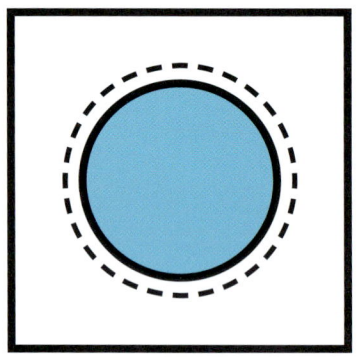

WORKING WITH FUSIBLE WEB

Once your shapes are traced onto the paper side of the fusible web, you are ready to cut them out. But resist the urge to cut right on the line just yet! Use a small, sharp pair of scissors to cut ⅛" to ¼" around the outside of the shape. After you adhere it to the back of the fabric (following the manufacturer's directions), cut on the line for a nice, crisp edge on your appliqué.

Does your fusible refuse to stick? It may have gotten old and dried out. Next time, store your fusible in a resealable bag to keep it fresh. If your appliqués fall off of the quilt while you're working, you can easily tack them back down with a fabric glue stick.

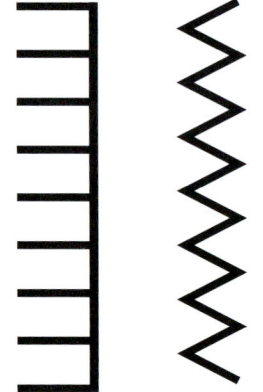

CHOOSING A MACHINE STITCH

Two great appliqué stitches for beginners are a blanket stitch and a zigzag stitch because you can easily work around a shape catching both the inside and outside of the fabric patch. Choose a stitch width that allows a little space between your zigs and your zags, because this is easier to control than a dense satin stitch. Before you stitch your fused pieces of fabric down, test the stitch you'd like to use on a scrap piece of fabric. You can then adjust it to your liking. **Tip:** Make sure to write down the setting you like or take a picture of it with your phone, so you can use the same setting for all of the appliqués in your project.

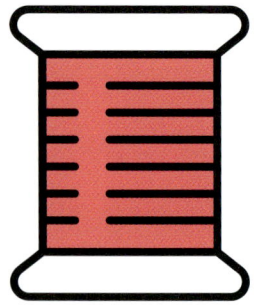

START SEWING

Before you start sewing down the appliqués, pull enough thread out of your machine so you can hold on to your thread tails. Starting with the needle down on a straight edge (if possible), begin machine stitching around the shape. Keep in mind, your stitch should just barely hit the background fabric.

IT'S NOT A RACE

Ready to move around the shape? Stitch slowly and guide the project through the machine using both hands. It's okay to start and stop many times when you sew around a curve. Just take it nice and easy!

WHAT'S THE POINT?

When you're stitching toward a point, sew right up to the shape and put your needle down at the tip of the point to make sure it's sewn down completely. Then use the needle up/down function (or your machine's handwheel) to stop with the needle down. Lift the presser foot and gently pivot your quilt to continue sewing. Remember to always pivot when your needle is on the outside edge. If you pivot before, you'll create a v-shaped gap in the stitching. Continue sewing.

TIE OFF ENDS

When you're finished sewing around the appliqué, stop your machine, and pull off some long thread tails before clipping the project off your machine. To bury your threads, thread a hand-sewing needle with both thread tails (self-threading needles work great), pull them through to the back of the quilt, and tie them off.

There you have it! Now that we've talked all about appliqué, I hope you have fun playing with fabric shapes in your projects. You're ready to stitch down your Dresdens and build beautiful quilts! And feel free to come back here when you need a little refresher.

DRESDEN TREE

Layered Dresdens build a beautiful Christmas tree. We love how the Dresden blades in various shades and prints give the tree depth and shine. Add a star to the top and ta-da! A tree you can hang wherever you are for the holidays!

materials

PROJECT SIZE
32" x 36"

- 2 packages of 5" print squares
- ¾ yard of background fabric
- (1) 5" brown print square
- (1) 5½" red print square
- ½ yard of bind
- 1¼ yards of backing fabric
- Missouri Star Large Dresden Plate Template for 10" Squares (template on page 211)
- Scrap of Heat n Bond fusible web
- A glue stick

Dresden Tree

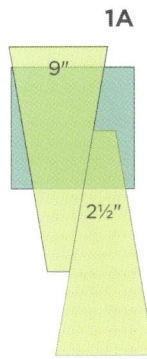

1A

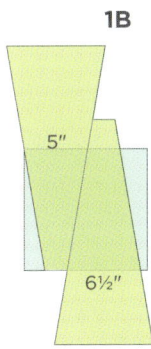

1B

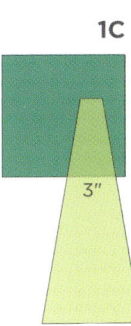

1C

STEP 1: CUT

From the background fabric, cut (1) 25½" strip across the width of the fabric. Subcut (1) 25½" x 29½" rectangle. Set the remaining fabric aside for another project.

Select (28) 5" print squares. Align the template with 1 edge of each square, as well as the line that indicates the size, and cut the following blades:

- 6 extra-large blades using the 9" mark. **1A**

- 5 extra-small blades using the 2½" mark. **1A**

- 15 medium blades using the 5" mark. **1B**

- 7 large blades using the 6½" mark. **1B**

- 7 small blades using the 3" mark. **1C**

Note: Cut the largest blades first and use the remaining scraps for the smaller blades.

STEP 1: CUT (CONTINUED)

Select (1) 5" print square for the star that goes at the treetop. Refer to *Put Your Own Spin On It* on page 22 to find the perfect 5-5½" circle for your project. Use the object to trace a circle and the star found on page 208 onto the paper side of the fusible. Rough cut the shapes from the fusible, then follow the manufacturer's instructions to adhere the circle to the reverse side of the 5½" red print square and the star to the reverse side of the 5" print square. Cut along the lines of each shape. Set aside until the tree has been constructed and sewn to the background fabric.

Follow the manufacturer's instructions to adhere the fusible to the back of a brown square. Cut (1) 2⅜" x 4¾" rectangle to make the tree trunk. Set aside for the moment.

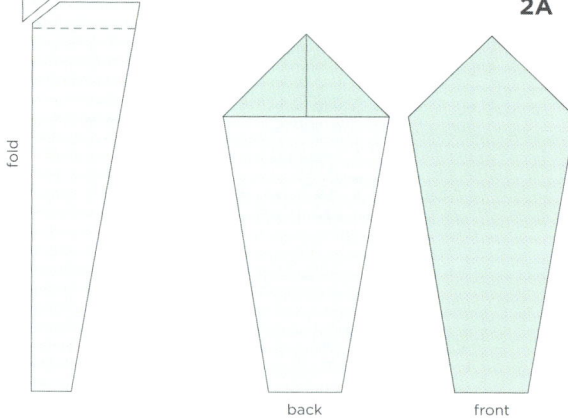

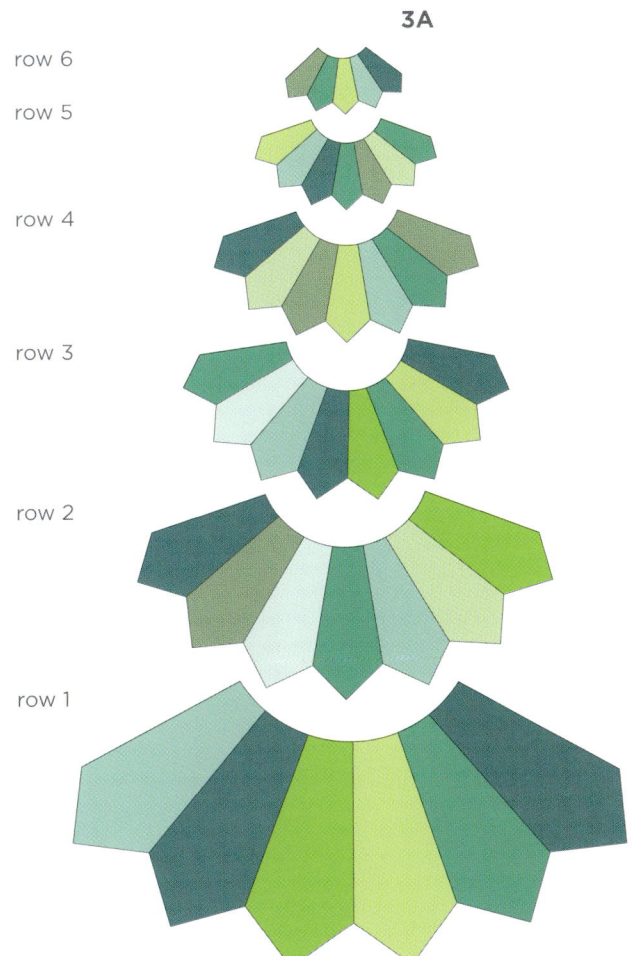

STEP 2: SEW

Make the tree branches by folding a blade in half lengthwise with right sides together. Stitch across the widest end of each blade. Trim the corner at an angle and turn right side out. Center the seam line and press. Repeat for all the blades. **2A**

STEP 3: MAKE THE ROWS

Sew the same-sized blades together into rows:

Row 1: 6 extra-large blades

Row 2: 7 large blades

Row 3: 8 medium blades

Row 4: 7 medium blades

Row 5: 7 small blades

Row 6: 5 extra-small blades

Turn the raw edge of the first and last blade of each row under ¼″ Press. **3A**

STEP 4: ASSEMBLE

Fold the background rectangle into quarters and lightly press the creases in place. Lay out the trunk and branches beginning with row 1 and work up toward the top of the tree. Use the pressed creases as guidelines to center each row.

When you are pleased with the arrangement, use the glue stick to temporarily adhere the branch rows to the background. Machine appliqué the elements in place using a blanket stitch or small zigzag.

Remove the paper backging from the circle and star, then position them on top of the tree. Follow the manufacturer's instructions to adhere in place. Machine appliqué using a zigzag or blanket stitch to complete the tree. **4A**

Press, then trim the background rectangle to 24½" x 28½".

4A

STEP 5: MAKE 4-PATCHES

Select (30) 5" squares. Pair up (2) 5" squares with right sides facing. Sew the 2 side seams together using a ¼" seam allowance. Measure 2½" in from the outer edge, and cut each pair in half. Open and press the seam allowance toward the darker fabric. **5A**

Align the seam allowances horizontally, then sew the units together end-to-end into a long strip. Avoid sewing 2 matching pieces together. **5B**

Fold over the first block of the strip at the seam line and cut at 2½" You will have (1) 2-patch unit and (1) 4-patch unit. Continue to fold and cut down the length of the strip. All cuts will yield a 4-patch unit except for the very first and last cuts. Those 2-patch units can be sewn into a 4-patch. **Make (30)** 4-patches. **5C**

STEP 6: PIECED BORDER

Sew a strip of (7) 4-patches together. Press. **Make 2**. Sew 1 to each side of the wall hanging center. Press. **6A**

STEP 7: QUILT & BIND

Refer to the finishing sections of *How to Create a Quilt* on pages 14-17 to quilt, square and trim, then add binding to finish. your project.

6A

1. Position Row 1 on the background fabric. Use a lapel stick to temporarily hold the row in place. Overlap Row 2.

2. Add and overlap Row 3.

3. Add Row 4 in the same manner.

4. Row 5 overlaps Row 4

5. Row 6 is the final row.

6. Top off the tree with the Star.

DRESDEN WREATH

With a single Dresden Plate, you can make a truly eye-catching and festive wreath for the holidays, or any other celebration on your calendar. There's also no appliqué circle for this project, so not only is it a breeze, but the peaked inner edges make it feel like a real wreath.

materials

PROJECT SIZE
28" X 28"

- 1 package of 5" squares
- ¾ yard of background fabric
- ½ yard of border fabric
- ½ yard of binding
- 1 yard of backing
- Missouri Star Large Dresden Plate Template for 10" Squares (template on page 211)

Dresden Wreath

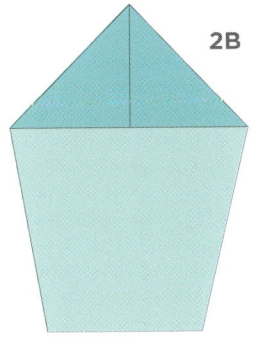

STEP 1: CUT

Select (36) 5″ print squares and set the remaining squares aside for another project.

Using the Dresden template, align the widest part of the template with the top of the squares, cut 36 blades.

From the background fabric cut (1) 24½″ strip across the width of the fabric. Subcut (1) 24½″ square. Set the remaining fabric aside for another project.

STEP 2: SEW

Fold a Dresden blade in half lengthwise, right sides facing. Sew across the wide end of the folded blade. **2A**

Clip the corner and turn the blade right side out. Poke the corner out and press with the seam in the center. Repeat to **make 20** blades. **2B**

Select 5 blades and sew them together along the long sides to form a 5 blade fan.* Press. Repeat to **make 4** fan units. Sew the 4 fan units together to make the outer wreath. Press. **2C 2D**

***Note**: Backstitch at the outside edge of each seam.

Fold the background fabric in half horizontally and vertically. Lightly crease the folds for placement purposes. Pin the wreath to the background fabric, aligning the seams of the 4 sections with the fold marks. **2E**

Fold the remaining 16 Dresden blades in half lengthwise, right sides facing. Sew across both ends of the blades.

Clip the corners and turn the blades right side out. Poke the corner out and press with the seam in the center. Repeat to **make 16** blades. **2F**

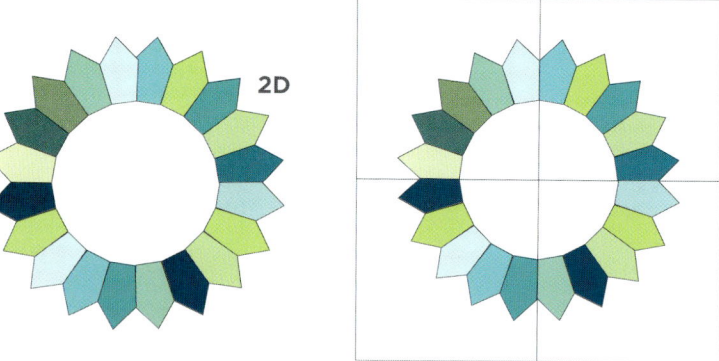

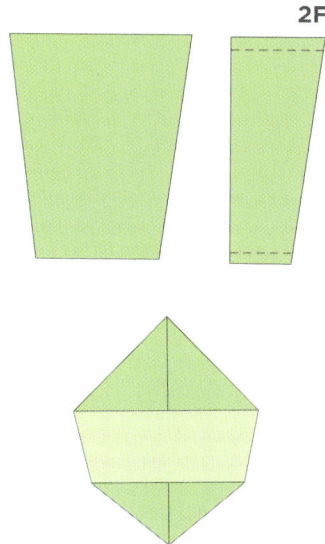

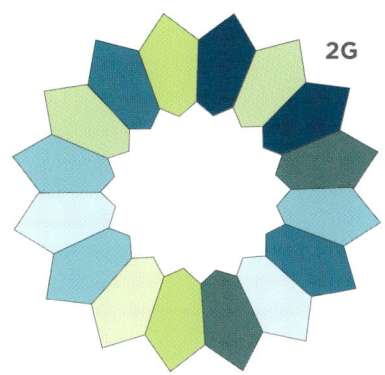

2G

2H

Sew the blades together into fan units as before. This time you will have 4 blades per fan unit. Sew the fan units together to make the inner wreath. **2G**

Place the inner wreath on top of the outer wreath and pin in place. Because this wreath has fewer blades, it should rest closer to the center of the piece. As you pin, make certain it lies flat. Don't hesitate to take a few seams in a bit if it's not flat.

Appliqué the smaller wreath in place using a blanket stitch on the outside and the inside edge. In the same manner, appliqué the outside wreath along the outer edge. **2H**

STEP 3: BORDER

Refer to diagram **3A** on the right for border reference. Cut (3) 2½" strips across the width of the fabric. Sew them together to make a long strip. Trim the borders from this strip. Measure, cut, and attach the borders to the project top. The approximate lengths are 24½" for the sides and 28½" for the top and bottom.

STEP 4: QUILT & BIND

Refer to the finishing sections of *How to Create a Quilt* on pages 14-17 to quilt, square and trim, then add binding to finish your project.

3A

1. Align the top of the Dresden template with the top of a 5″ square. Cut the shape.

2. Sew across the top of each of 20 blades.

3. Open the blade and press the piece flat.

4. When making the inner wreath pieces, sew across both ends of each blade.

5. Open the piece and press the points flat.

6. Layer the outer and inner rings of the wreath onto the background fabric. Stitch in place using a blanket stitch.

BLOOM AND GROW

With three Dresden Plates, you can easily create this lovely Dresden flower pot. We went with this beautiful collection for ours, and we're not at all blue about how it turned out! Bloom and Grow your own attractive Dresden plant to hang anywhere in your home.

materials

PROJECT SIZE
28" x 38"

- 2 packages of 5" print squares
- ¼ yard stems and leaves fabric
- (1) 10" print sware for pot
- ¾ yard of background fabric
- ½ yard of binding
- 1 yard of backing
- ½ yard of fusable interfacing
- Missouri Star Large Dresden Plate Template for 10" Squares (template on page 211)

Bloom and Grow

1A

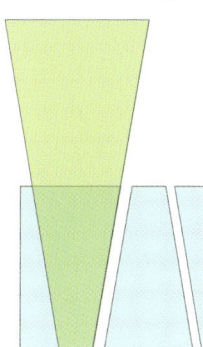

1B

1C

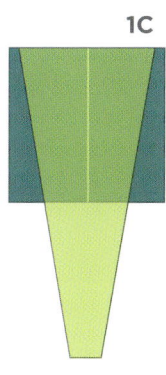

STEP 1: CUT

From the background yardage cut (1) 24½" x 36½" rectangle.

All the "petals" for the flowers are cut using the Dresden template. Keep the petals for each flower together.

For the small flower, select (3) 5" print squares and cut them in half. Use the 2½" mark on the ruler to cut 3 blades from each rectangle, rotating the template 180° after each cut. You will need a **total of 18** small petals. **1A**

For the medium flower, select (10) 5" print squares. Use the 5" mark on the template to cut 2 petals from each square, rotating the template 180° after each cut. You will need a **total of 20** medium petals. **1B**

For the large flower, select (10) 5" print squares. Press a crease down the middle of each square. Align the ruler's center to the fold. Set the wide top of the ruler on 1 side. Mark the width of the ruler. Slide the ruler up, setting the ruler's narrow edge on the opposite side. Mark the width of the ruler's narrow tip, keeping it centered on the fold. Connect the marks on each side and cut along those lines. You will need a **total of 10** large petals. **1C**

STEP 1: CUT (CONTINUED)

From the stem fabric, cut (1) 2½" strip across the width. Subcut (3) 2½" x 5" rectangles. Use the Dresden template to cut a **total of 3** leaves. **1D**

Cut (17) 5" print squares in half for a **total of (34)** 2½" x 5" rectangles and set them aside for the pieced border and picket fence. **1E**

Set the 2 remaining print squares aside for another project.

Note: For an optional bottom border, cut (1) 5" square from the remaining stem fabric. Cut this square and the remaining (2) 5" print squares in half for a **total of (40)** 2½" x 5" rectangles and set them aside for the pieced border.

STEP 2: SEW THE POINTS

Fold a petal in half lengthwise, right sides facing. Sew across the wide end of the folded blade. **2A**

Clip the corner at the fold and turn the blade right side out. Gently poke the corner out and press with the seam in the center. **2B**

Repeat for all flower petals, leaves, and for 12 of the 2½" x 5" rectangles. **2C 2D 2E 2F**

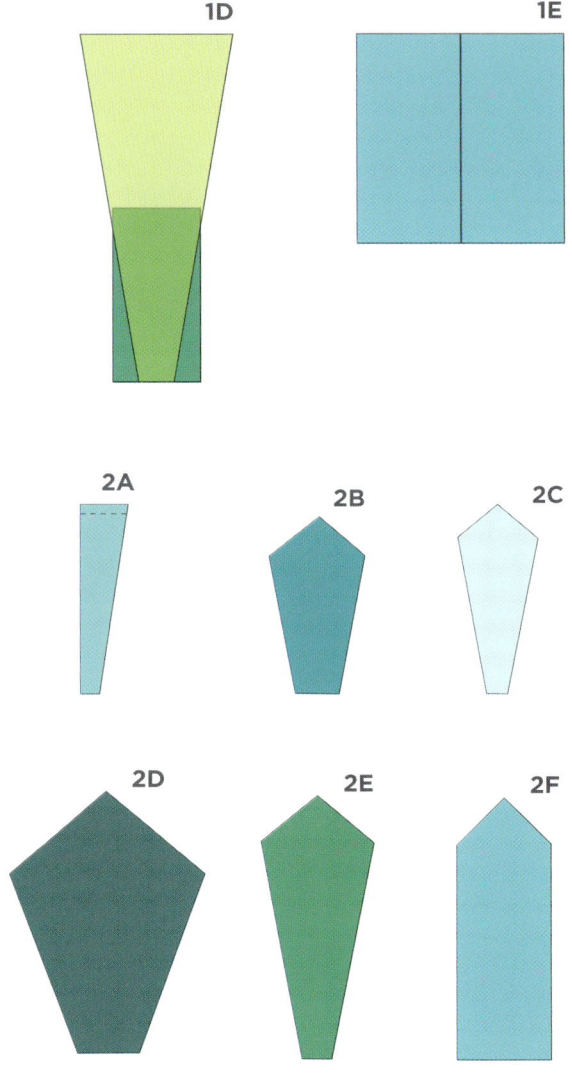

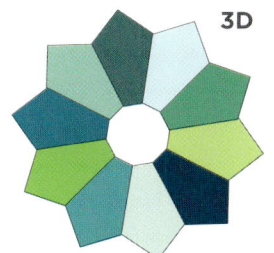

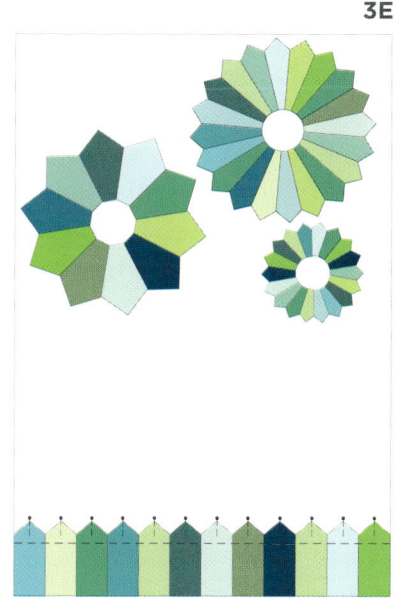

STEP 3: FENCE & FLOWERS

Sew the 12 "pickets" together in a row using a ¼" seam allowance. Press the seams to 1 side in the same direction. **3A**

In the same manner, sew the 18 small petals together in a circle to create the small flower. Press in 1 direction. **3B**

Sew the 20 medium petals together in a circle to create the medium flower. Press in 1 direction. **3C**

Sew the 10 large petals together in a circle to create the large flower. Press in 1 direction. **3D**

Position the picket fence along the bottom 24½" side of the background rectangle, so that the points of the picket just cover the raw edge of the rectangle. Baste the fence to the background along the rectangle's edge at ⅛". Pin the picket points. **3E**

Refer to diagram **3E** to arrange the flowers on the background rectangle and pin in place.

STEP 4: POT & CENTERS

From the binding fabric:
- Cut (4) 2½" strips across the width of the fabric. Set these aside for binding.

- 3 circles for flower centers. Refer to *Put your own spin on it* on page 22 to find the perfect size of circle for your project. **Note**: Remember to add a ¼" seam allowance if you want the circle the same size as your object

From the fusible interfacing:
- Cut (1) 10" strip across the width. Subcut (1) 10" square.

- Cut 3 circles the same size as the fabric circles you cut.

Lay the 10" interfacing square atop the 10" print square. Measure and mark 2" from both sides along the bottom edge. Draw a line from the top left corner to the 2" mark on the left side. Repeat for the right side. Cut along both lines to have a pot shape from interfacing and from the print square. **4A**

Cut a slit for turning in each interfacing piece. **4B**

Lay an interfacing circle atop the same size print circle with the glue (bumpy) side of the interfacing next to the right side of the print. Sew around the perimeter using a ¼" seam allowance. Turn right sides out though the slit. Push out the edges. *Do not press!* Repeat with each interfacing/print pair of circles. **4C**

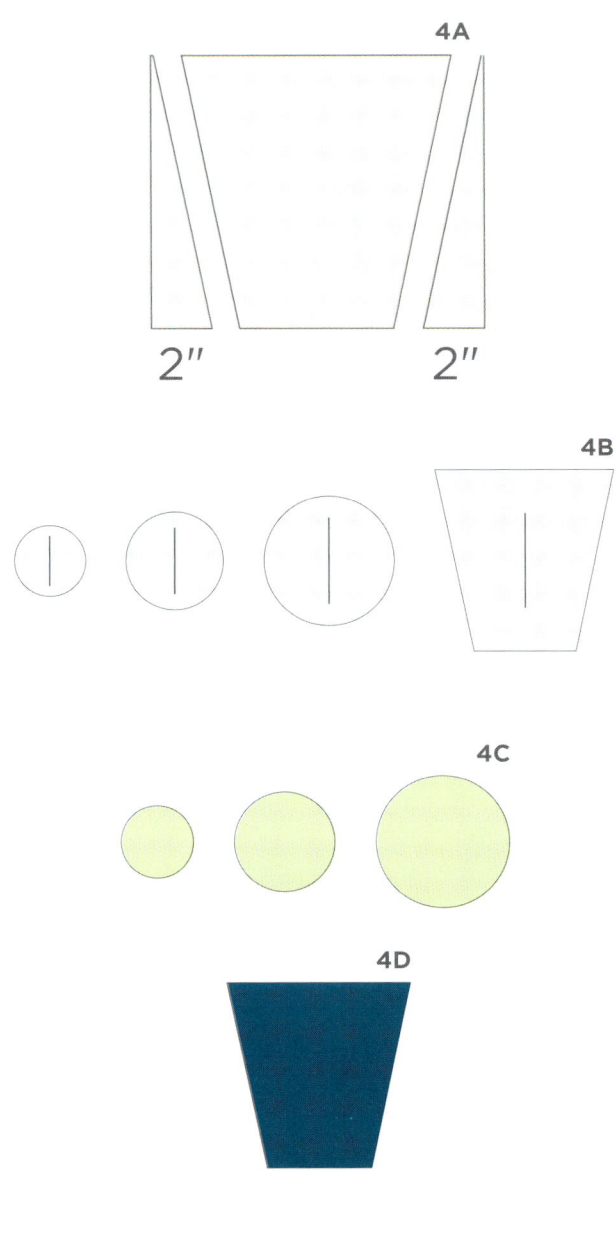

5A

5B

Repeat with the interfacing and print pot. Clip the corners and turn right sides out. Push out the corners. *Do not press!* **4D**

Refer to the diagram **5A** to arrange the pot and flower centers right side up atop the background rectangle. Pin into place.

STEP 5: STEMS & LEAVES

Iron the 2½" stem strip in half lengthwise. Determine the position and length of each stem. Add an extra ½" to your measurement so that the raw ends will tuck ¼" beneath the flower and the pot. **Cut 3** stems.

Use a pencil to trace along the raw edge of the stem. **Cut 3** stems. **5A**

Place each leaf with the raw end beyond the marked line. This way they will be covered by the stem's seam. **Note**: You may wish to trim some of your leaves shorter. Pin in place. **5A**

With the long raw edge of the stem placed along the marked line, sew a ¼" seam, fully covering the ends of the leaves as you go. Make sure the short ends are covered by a flower and the pot. Fold the stem strip over the raw edge encasing it. **5B**

STEP 6: APPLIQUÉ

When you are happy with your arrangement, carefully remove the pins from the flower centers and pot only, then follow the manufacturer's instructions to fuse those pieces in place.

Appliquè *all* the elements into place by hand or machine: stems first, then leaves, picket points, flower petals, flower centers and flower pot. A blanket, straight, or zigzag stitch is recommended for machine applique. *See All About Dresden Appliqué on page 88.* **6A**

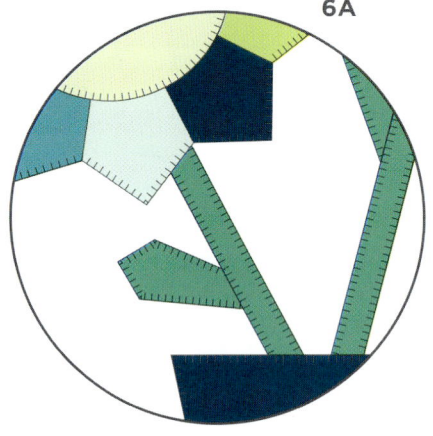

STEP 7: PIECED BORDER

From the remaining rectangles, sew 8 rectangles end-to-end. Press. **Make 2**. Refer to diagram **7A** to the left to attach 1 to both sides of your quilt center. Trim any excess.

Sew 6 rectangles together end-to-end and press. Refer to diagram **7A** to the left to sew the pieced border to the top of the quilt center and trim the edges. Press.

Note: For the optional bottom border, sew the 6 remaining rectangles together end-to-end and press. Refer to diagram **7B** to the left to sew the pieced border to the bottom of the quilt center and trim the edges. Press.

STEP 8: QUILT & BIND

Refer to the finishing sections of *How to Create a Quilt* on pages 14-17 to quilt, square and trim, then add binding to finish your project.

1. After sewing across the widest side, clip the folded corner to reduce the bulk.

2. Gently poke the corner out.

3. Press with the seam in the center.

4. Sew the 20 medium petals together in a circle to create the medium flower. Press 1 direction.

5. Lay an interfacing circle atop the same size print circle with the glue (bumpy) side of the interfacing next to the right side of the print. Sew around the perimeter. Turn right sides out though the slit. Push out the edges. Do not press!

6. With the long raw edge of the stem placed along the marked line, sew a ¼" seam, fully capturing the ends of the leaves as you go. The short ends are covered by a flower and the pot. Fold the stem strip over the raw edge encasing it.

SPRING DRESDENS RUNNER

By sewing Dresdens into this simple fan of succulents and leaves you can create a beautiful table runner! Spring is in full swing with this Dresden flowered masterpiece! With basic piecing in the middle to leave room for your centerpiece, you'll have a gorgeous project for any tablescape.

materials

PROJECT SIZE
40½" x 13½"

- 1 package of 5" print squares
- ¼ yard of complimentary print fabric
- ½ yard of background fabric or (2) 10" squares
- ½ yard of binding

- ¾ yard of backing
- ¼ yard or (2) 5" squares of fusible interfacing
- Missouri Star Large Dresden Plate Template for 10" Squares (template on page 211)

Spring Dresdens

STEP 1: CUT

From the complimentary print fabric cut:
- (3) 2½" strips across the width of the fabric.
  - From (2) strips subcut a **total of (4)** 2½" x 14" rectangles.
  - From the remaining strip subcut a **total of (4)** 2½" x 10" rectangles.

From the background fabric cut:
- (1) 10" strip across the width of the fabric.
  - Subcut (2) 10" squares and set the rest of the fabric aside for another project.

From the fusible interfacing cut:
- (1) 5" strip across the width of the fusible interfacing.
  - Subcut (2) 5" squares.

STEP 2: MAKE THE DRESDEN FLOWERS

Select (10) 5" print squares for the Dresden flower blades. Lay a 5" print square right side up. Place the template on the edge of the bottom of the square. Cut 1 blade*. Repeat to cut 1 blade from each of the print squares. **2A**

***Note**: 2 blades can be cut from (1) 5" square, but we chose 10 different prints for the petals.

STEP 2: MAKE THE DRESDEN FLOWERS (CONTINUED)

Fold 1 wedge in half lengthwise with right sides facing. Stitch straight across the larger end. Trim the corner, turn the blade right side out, and gently poke out the point. Press, centering the seam. **Make 10**. **2B 2C**

Sew 5 petals together side-by-side using a ¼" seam allowance. Press seams to the same side. Turn the raw edges of both sides under ¼" and press. Repeat to **make 2** Dresden flowers. **2D**

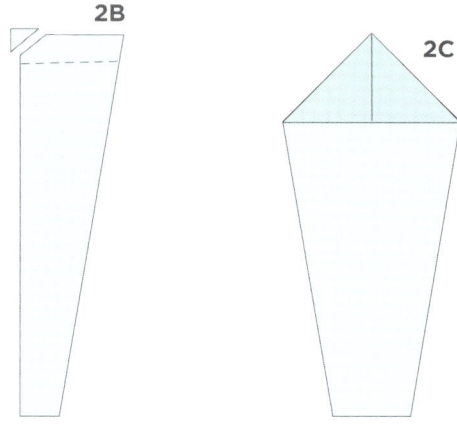

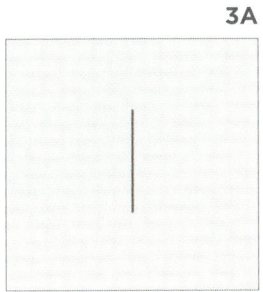

3A

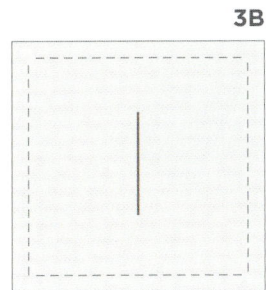

3B

3C

STEP 3: MAKE THE FLOWER POTS

Cut a slit for turning in each interfacing square. **3A**

Lay 1 fusible square, adhesive-side down, on top of the right side of (1) 5″ print square. Sew all the way around the square with a ¼″ seam allowance.

Turn right sides out though the slit. Push out the edges. **Do not press!** Repeat with a second interfacing/print pair of squares. **3B 3C**

STEP 4: POT THE FLOWERS

Fold a 10″ background square in half once and press. Line up the middle of the Dresden flower to the folded line with the flower ⅞″ from the top of the background square. When you are happy with the placement pin or glue the flowers into place. **4A**

Appliqué the flower into place along its sides and zigzag points using a blanket, straight or zigzag stitch. **4B**

Lay a pot so it sits on the bottom of the square and covers the bottom raw-edges of the flowers. Fuse into place. Appliqué around the pot in the same manner as the flowers. **Make 2**. **4C**

Block Size: 10″ unfinished, 9½″ unfinished

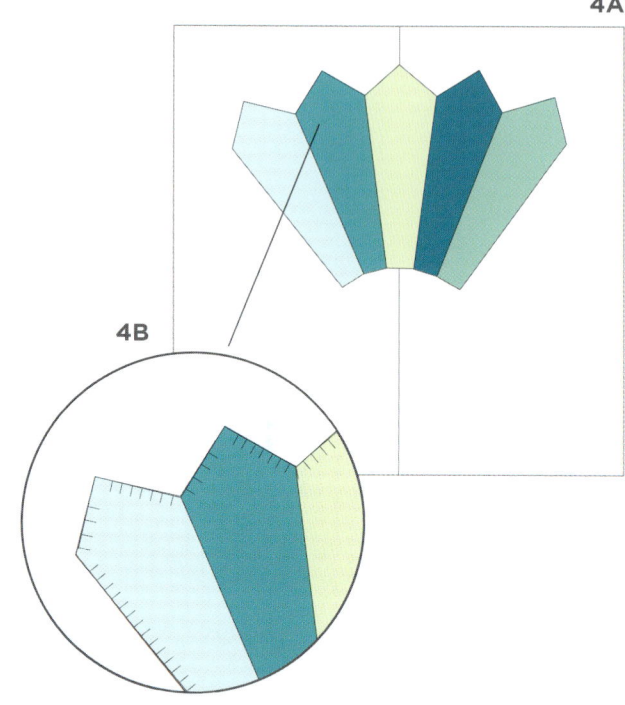

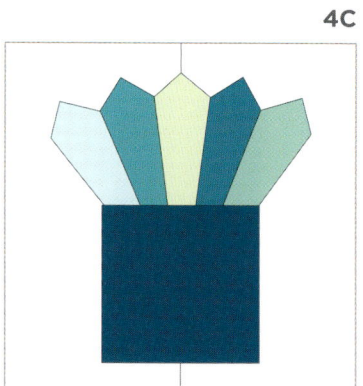

STEP 5: BORDER

Pick up the complimentary print rectangles you cut in Step 1. Sew a 2½" x 10" rectangle to both sides of the block. Press. Sew a 2½" x 14" rectangle to the top and bottom of the block. Press. **5A**

Bordered Block Size: 14" unfinished, 13½" finished

STEP 6: MAKE THE CENTER BLOCK

Select (12) 5" print squares for the center of the table runner. Set the remaining print squares aside for another project.

Arrange the print squares in **3 rows of 4**. Sew the squares together to form rows. Press the rows in opposite directions. Nest the seams and sew the rows together. Press. **6A**

Center Block Size: 18½" x 14" unfinished, 18" x 13½" finished

STEP 7: ARRANGE & SEW

Place a bordered block on either side of the center block as shown. Sew the blocks together. Press. **7A**

STEP 8: QUILT & BIND

Refer to the finishing sections of *How to Create a Quilt* on pages 14-17 to quilt, square and trim, then add binding to finish your project.

7A

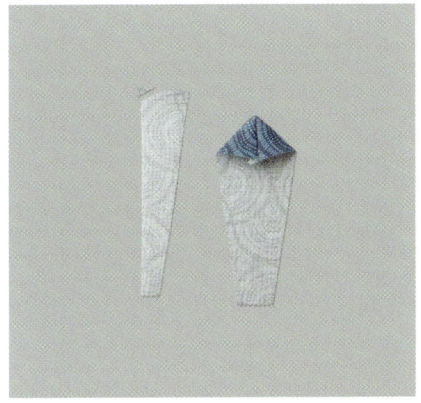

1. Fold 1 wedge in half lengthwise with right sides facing. Stitch straight across the larger end. Trim the corner, turn the blade right side out, and gently poke out the point. Press, centering the seam. Make 10.

2. Sew 5 different petals together using a ¼" seam allowance. Press seams to the same side. Turn the raw edges of both sides under ¼" and press. Repeat to make 2 Dresden flowers.

3. Cut a slit for turning in each interfacing square. Lay 1 fusible square, adhesive-side down, on top of the right side of (1) 5" print square. Sew all the way around the square with a ¼" seam allowance. Turn right sides out though the slit. Push out the edges. Do not press! Repeat with a second interfacing/print pair of squares.

4. Fold a 10" background square in half once and press. Line up the middle of the Dresden flower to the folded line with the flower ⅞" from the top of the background square.

5. Appliqué the flower into place along its sides and zigzag points using a blanket, straight or zigzag stitch. Place a pot so it sits on the bottom of the background square and covers the bottom raw-edges of the flowers. Fuse into place. Appliqué around the sides and top of the pot in the same manner as the flowers. Make 2.

JOSH'S STAR

We love asking "What if?" and Jenny's son, Josh, created this star quilt answering that question. What if we used the dresden template to create a star shape in this easier-than-it-looks block? It looks quite complicated to craft, but nothing could be further from the truth!

materials

QUILT SIZE
73" x 73"

- 1 package of 10" print squares
- 1 yard of sashing and inner border fabric
- 1¼ yards of outer border fabric
- ¾ yard of binding
- 4½ yards of backing - vertical seam(s)
- Missouri Star Large Dresden Plate Template for 10" Squares (template on page 211)

Josh's Star

STEP 1: CUT

From the sashing fabric, cut:
- (6) 2½" strips across the width of the fabric.
  - Subcut 3 strips into a **total of (5)** 2½" x 18½" rectangles.

- Set the remaining fabric aside for the inner border.

STEP 2: SEW

Select 20 medium to dark print squares.

Layer 2 squares together with right sides facing. Sew on 2 opposite sides of the squares. **2A**

Measure 5" in from the outer sewn edge to the center of the sewn squares. Cut in half vertically. Press towards the darker fabric. **2B**

Select 20 light to medium/light squares. Sew on 2 opposite sides of the squares as before. Measure in 5" from the edge and cut in half vertically. Press towards the darker fabric. **2C**

Align the long edge of the template along the bottom of a pieced rectangle. Cut along the edge of the template. You will have a two-toned blade shape. Repeat for all the pieced rectangles. **2D**

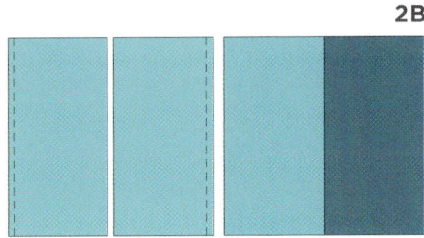

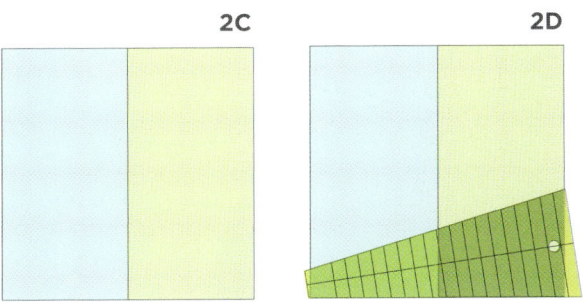

STEP: 2 SEW (CONTINUED)

Stack the light blades together and place the darker blades in another stack.

With right sides facing, sew a light blade shape to a darker rectangle that has been trimmed. **Note**: As you align the 2 pieces that the blade shape is slightly offset by about ¼″ Press. **Make 20** quadrants with light blades and dark trimmed rectangles. Square to 9½″ as necessary. **2E**

Arrange 4 quadrants as shown. Sew the quadrants together in rows and press in opposite directions. Nest the seams and sew the rows together. Press. **Make 5** blocks with light blades and dark trimmed rectangles. **2F**

Follow the instructions above and sew a dark blade to a lighter trimmed rectangle. **2G**

Repeat the previous instructions to **make 4** blocks with dark blades and light trimmed rectangles. **2H**

Block Size: 18½″ unfinished, 18″ finished

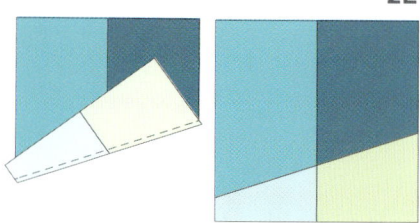

2E

2F

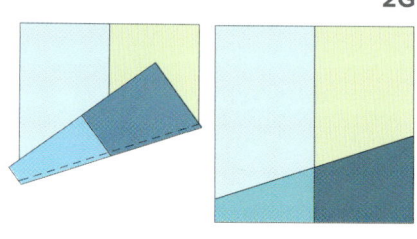

2G

2H

STEP 3: ARRANGE & SEW

Refer to diagram **3A** on the left to lay out the blocks in **3 rows of 3** as shown. Add a 2½" x 18½" rectangle between each block. Sew the blocks and rectangles into rows and press towards the rectangles.

Take the (3) 2½" strips set aside earlier and sew them together in 1 long strip. Trim the horizontal sashing from this strip. Measure the length of your rows and trim 2 horizontal sashing strips to your measurement, approximately 58½".

Sew the rows together, adding a horizontal sashing strip between each row. Press towards the sashing.

STEP 4: INNER BORDER

Cut (7) 2½" strips across the width of the inner border fabric. Sew the strips together to make a long strip. Trim the borders from this strip. Refer to diagram **4A** to the left for the inner and outer borders. The lengths are approximately 58½" for the sides and approximately 62½" for the top and bottom.

STEP 5: OUTER BORDER

Cut (7) 6" strips across the width of the outer border fabric. Sew the strips together to make a long strip. Trim the borders from this strip. Measure, cut, and attach the outer borders to the quilt top. The lengths are approximately 62½" for the sides and approximately 73½" for the top and bottom. **5A**

STEP 6: QUILT & BIND

Refer to the finishing sections of *How to Create a Quilt* on pages 14-17 to quilt, square and trim, then add binding to finish your quilt.

5A

1. Layer a medium 10″ square with a dark 10″ square with right sides facing. Sew on 2 adjacent sides of the squares using a ¼″ seam allowance.

2. Measure 5″ in from the outer edge of the sewn squares. Cut in half vertically. Open and press the seam allowance toward the darker fabric. Repeat, using light to medium light squares.

3. Align the long edge of the Dresden Plate template along the bottom of a pieced rectangle. Cut along the edge of the template to make a two-toned wedge shape. Repeat for all pieced rectangles.

4. Sew a light wedge to a darker rectangle that has been trimmed. Make 4 quadrants and sew them together to complete one block.

5. Sew a dark wedge to a lighter rectangle that has been trimmed. Make 4 quadrants and sew them together to complete 1 block.

DRESDEN COIN

Toss a coin to your Dresden and watch them stack! Simple, elegant and most innovative, this project uses Dresdens by alternating cuts to create a straightened pattern. You really won't believe how easy this one comes together, and you'll be pleased as pie every time you see it hanging on your wall or draped over your couch. Note: This quilt inspired a peiced border! Learn more on page 150.

materials

QUILT SIZE
74½" x 79"

- 1 package of 10" print squares
- 1¼ yards of sashing fabric - includes inner border
- ½ yard of fabric for middle border
- 2 yards of outer border fabric - includes fabric for additonal blades in the quilt top
- ¾ yards of binding fabric
- 5 yards of backing - vertical seam(s) or 2½ yards of backing 108" wide
- 2 yrd of Heat n Bond - Feather weight fusible interfacing
- ¼ yard of fusible interfacing
- Missouri Star Large Dresden Plate Template for 10" Squares (template on page 211)

Dresden Coin

STEP 1: CUT

Use the template to cut 3 blades from each 10" print square in your package. Rotate the template 180° as you cut the blades. **1A**

From the outer border fabric, cut (3) 10" strips across the width of the fabric. Use template to subcut 15 blades from 2 of the strips and 4 blades from the last strip. Add these to the blades cut previously for a **total of 160**. Cut the remaining strip into (2) 5" wide strips and set these strips aside for the outer border.

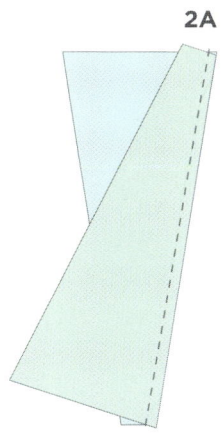

STEP 2: CHAIN PIECE

Chain piecing is a quick method of sewing blocks together. Layer 2 blades, right sides together, thin end to thick end. Make sure the 2 pieces are offset slightly so the shorter edges of the blades will line up with each other after sewing them together. **2A**

Feed the pair through the sewing machine. Continue sewing off the fabric a few stitches and feed the next pair through the machine and so on.

Snip threads to separate units. Press. Next sew 4 together, then 8, 16, and 32. **Make 5** columns of 32 blades each.

STEP 3: STRAIGHTEN

Straighten both ends of each coin column using the template. Match the center line on the ruler to the last seam. Be careful to place the ruler correctly—the wide end should be the same direction as the last blade. Cut to straighten. **3A**

3A

STEP 4: SASHING

Cut (13) 3" strips across the width of the sashing fabric. Sew the strips together to make 1 long strip. Measure the length of the 5 columns. Trim 4 sashing strips to the length of your columns, approximately 59½" Set the remainder of the strip aside for the inner border.

Refer to diagram **4A** to arrange your 5 columns with a sashing strip in between. Sew the columns and sashing strips together and press toward the sashing.

4A

5A

STEP 5: INNER BORDER

Pick up the remainder of the strip made for the sashing. Trim the borders from this strip. Measure, cut, and attach the inner borders to the quilt top. The lengths are approximately 59½" for the sides and 70½" for the top and bottom. **5A**

STEP 6: MIDDLE BORDER

Cut (7) 2" strips across the width of the middle border fabric. Sew the strips together to make 1 long strip. Trim the borders from this strip. Measure, cut, and attach the middle borders to the quilt top. The lengths are approximately 67½" for the sides and 66" for the top and bottom.

STEP 7: OUTER BORDER

Cut (7) 5" strips across the width of the outer border fabric. Combine these with the (2) strips set aside earlier and sew the strips together to make 1 long strip. Trim the borders from this strip. Measure, cut, and attach the outer borders to the quilt top. The lengths are approximately 70½" for the sides and 75" for the top and bottom. **7A**

STEP 8: QUILT & BIND

Refer to the finishing sections of *How to Create a Quilt on pages* 14-17 to quilt, square and trim, then add binding to finish your quilt.

7A

1 Use the large Dresden template to cut 3 blades from each 10″ print square in your package. Rotate the template 180° as you cut the blades.

2 Layer 2 blades, right sides together, thin end to thick end. Make sure the 2 pieces are offset slightly so the shorter edges of the blades will line up with each other after sewing them together. Make 80 blade pairs.

3 Sew the blade pairs together into 5 rows of 32 blades.

4 Straighten both ends of each coin column using the template. Match the center line on the ruler to the last seam. Be careful to place the ruler correctly—it faces the same direction as the last blade. Cut to straighten.

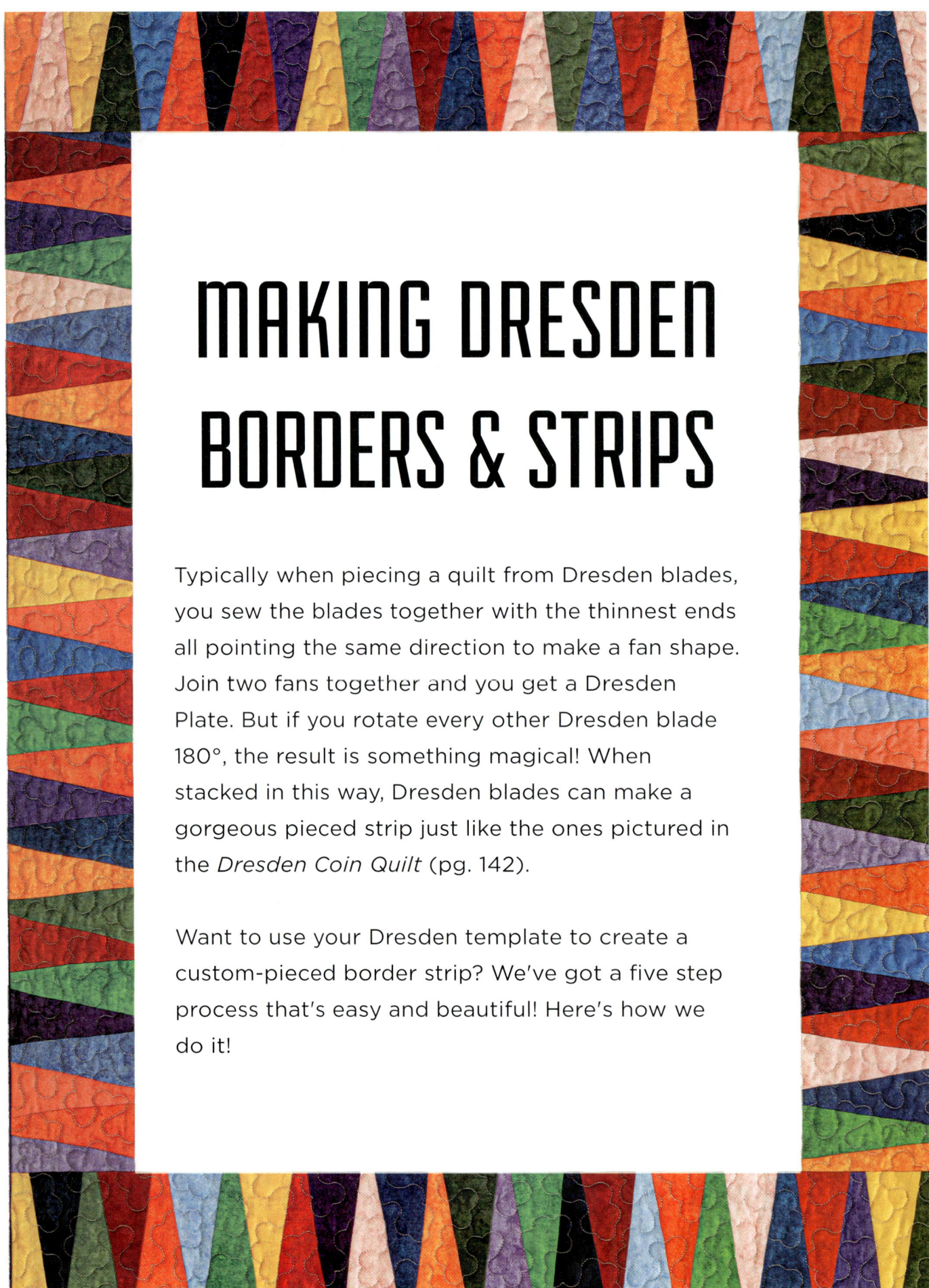

MAKING DRESDEN BORDERS & STRIPS

Typically when piecing a quilt from Dresden blades, you sew the blades together with the thinnest ends all pointing the same direction to make a fan shape. Join two fans together and you get a Dresden Plate. But if you rotate every other Dresden blade 180°, the result is something magical! When stacked in this way, Dresden blades can make a gorgeous pieced strip just like the ones pictured in the *Dresden Coin Quilt* (pg. 142).

Want to use your Dresden template to create a custom-pieced border strip? We've got a five step process that's easy and beautiful! Here's how we do it!

1 CHOOSE A SIZE

Do you prefer your borders to be thin, thicker, or extra-wide? The Missouri Star Large Dresden Template for 10" Squares is conveniently marked with cutting lines every half-inch from 1" to 10". This means you can easily choose any Dresden border width you prefer, finished up to 9½" wide!

For example, if you want to make a pieced border that's 4" wide in your finished quilt, you'd cut the Dresden blades at 4½". This extra ½" will disappear in the seam allowance (¼ inch seam allowance on each side of the border). Voila!

Pieced border finished width + ½" seam allowance = Dresden blade cut size

2 CUT THE BLADES

Now, how do you know the number of blades to cut for a border? That's easy! You'll need to first cut and sew together 2 Dresden blades as shown, then measure the width across both blades when joined.

Take that measurement, and subtract a seam allowance of ½" inch to get the finished measurement of the 2-blade section.

Q – ½" = X (finished width of 2-blade section)

Next, measure your quilt top to determine the length needed for each of your border strips, starting with the left and right sides.

Y = border length needed

CUT THE BLADES (CONTINUED)

Finally, take Y and divide by X. Now double that number. Add 2 and round up to the nearest whole number. This will give you the number of blades needed per side border.

2(Y/X) + 2 = Z (number of blades needed per side)

If your 2 blades together measure 6" wide, then subtract your ½" seam allowance and you get 5½". If your side border length is 60" then you'll divide 60" by 5½" and you get 10.9.

Now we need to multiply 10.9 by 2 (2 blades for each 5½" section, remember?) and we get 21.8. Add 2 more blades (one for either end of the border) and we have 23.8. Round up to 24!

Our formula looks likethis: 2(60"/5.5") + 2 = 23.8 rounded up to 24. (Remember, we have to double the result of (Y/X)—since each section contains 2 blades—and add 2 extra blades to get the total number of blades needed per side border.)

Cut 24 blades for the right side and 24 for the left side for a **total of 48** blades for the side border strips.

SEW THE SIDE BORDERS

Stack and sew those blades together as shown in the *Dresden Coin Quilt* (pg. 142) to make the border strips. Center a border strip to each side of the quilt. Then sew, press, and trim as needed. **Tip:** Make sure to pin the borders to the quilt top before sewing them on. You'll want to avoid stretching the pieced fabric as you attach it.

4 ADD THE TOP & BOTTOM BORDERS

Next, measure the width of the quilt top (including the border strips you just added) to determine Y for the top and the bottom border strips. Using the formula again, calculate the number of blades needed for the top and bottom border strips.

5 SHOW IT OFF

Clearly, we love Dresden quilts. But did you know that you can put a Dresden border on ANY quilt? For instance…

- You can dress up a panel into a cute baby quilt in a snap!
- Add a fun, colorful border to a quilt featuring stars, squares, or triangles to echo those interesting shapes.
- Quickly increase the size of a table or bed runner…voila!

When planning a border from Dresden blades, you may also want to frame it with thin solid borders on either side. This will set it apart from the quilt top and really let it pop. There's also fabric placement to consider. For instance, will you place the blades in a planned color order or go with a more improvisational arrangement?

Finally, this is one of our favorite time savers when it comes to sewing a Dresden border. Cut full-length Dresden blades using the 10" template. Piece them together as we described for the borders. After pressing the full-width border, cut it in half lengthwise to make 2 half-width border strips! This shaves serious time off of your cutting and sewing of the borders.

DRESDEN SQUARED RUNNER

A simple change can make a noticeable and exciting twist on a classic. By squaring up the classic Dresden Plate and adding a thin sashing, you can create an amazing table runner that looks gorgeous in any kitchen or dining room, or at the foot of your bed. Check out the easy steps to finish the continued Dresden border, and pretty soon you'll be all squared away!

materials

PROJECT SIZE
52½" x 21½"

- 1 package of 10" print sqares
- ¾ yard of fabric for sashing, circles and the border
- ½ yard of binding fabric
- 1½ yard of backing - vertical seam(s)
- Missouri Star Large Dresden Plate Template for 10" Squares (template on page 211)
- ¼ yard of fusible interfacing

Dresden Squared Runner

STEP 1: CUT

Select the lightest 10" print square and set it aside for the moment.

Select (20) 10" print squares and set the remaining squares aside for another project.
- Using the template, cut 3 blades from each selected square, rotating the template 180° after each cut. You will need a **total of 60** blades. **1A**

From the sashing fabric cut:
- (1) 4" strip across the width of the fabric.
  - Subcut (3) 4" squares.

- (5) 1½" strips across the width of the fabric.
  - From 4 strips subcut (2) 1½" x 16" rectangles and (1) 1½" x 10" rectangle.

  - From the remaining strip subcut (2) 1½" x 10" rectangles. Add these to the rectangles cut earlier for a **total of (8)** 1½" x 16" sashing rectangles and a **total of (6)** 1½" x 10" sashing rectangles.

- Set the remaining fabric aside for another project.

From the Heat n Bond cut:
- (1) 4" strip across the width of the fusible.
  - Subcut (3) 4" squares.

- Set the remaining Heat n Bond aside for another project.

1A

STEP 2: BLOCK CONSTRUCTION

Join 20 blades to make a Dresden plate. Begin sewing at the top of the blade, backstitch, then stop at the bottom. Press all seams to 1 side. **Make 3**. **2A**

Fold the 10" light print square you set aside earlier in half vertically and horizontally. Press to form creases. Center the light square atop a Dresden plate, lining up the creases with the sewn seams. **2B**

Using the square as a guide, place a long ruler along 1 edge of the square and trim the Dresden circle. Repeat to trim along the other side of the square. Move the sides out of the way and trim the top and bottom. **2C**

Cut a 2½" pieced strip from the long edge of each piece you just trimmed. Keep the strips next to their coinciding fabrics on the 10" center unit. **2D**

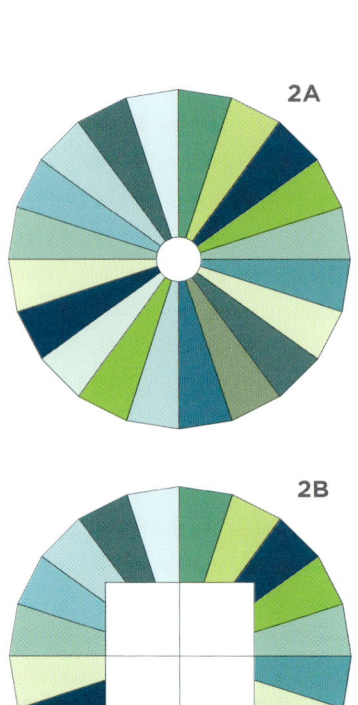
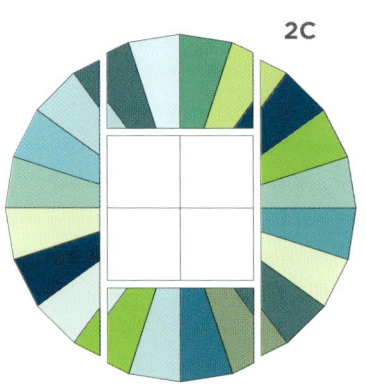
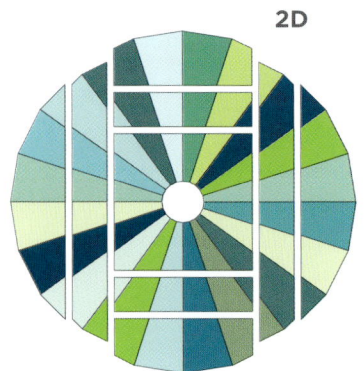

2E

2F

Sew a 1½″ x 10″ sashing rectangle to the top and bottom of the unit. Sew the coinciding pieced strip to the top and bottom. Press. **2E**

Sew a 1½″ x 16″ sashing rectangle to both sides of the unit. Press. **2F**

Line up the center seams and sew the coinciding pieced strips to both sides of the unit. Press. Trim the ends of the pieced strips even with the top and bottom. **Make 3**. **2G**

Block Size: 16″ unfinished, 15½″ finished

2G

STEP 3: ADD CENTER CIRCLES

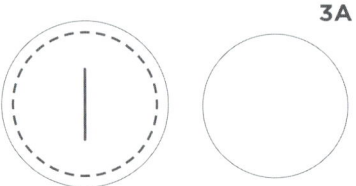
3A

Refer to *Put Your Own Spin On It* on page 22 to find the perfect 4-4½" circle for your project. Use the object to trace 3 circles onto the fusible interfacing and 1 circle on each 4" sashing fabric square. Cut out each circle.

Cut a 3" slit in an interfacing circle. Layer the interfacing circle with a sashing fabric circle, right sides facing. **Note**: The bumpy side of the fusible interfacing will be facing the right side of the fabric circle. Sew ¼" inside the outer edge. **3A**

Turn the circles right side out. Press a circle* to the center of each block and appliqué in place using a zigzag, blanket, or decorative stitch. **3B**

***Tip**: before pressing the circle to the center, lay either a pressing cloth or a piece of freezer paper between your block and the ironing board.

3B

4A

STEP 4: ARRANGE & SEW

Sew the blocks together into **1 row of 3** with a 1½" x 16" sashing rectangle between each of the blocks. Press. **4A**

STEP 5: BORDER

Use the (3) 2½" strips you set aside earlier and sew them together to make 1 long strip. Trim the borders from this strip. Measure, cut, and attach the borders to the project top. The top and bottom borders are sewn first. The strips are approximately 49" for the top and bottom and 20" for the sides. **5A**

STEP 6: QUILT & BIND

Refer to the finishing sections of *How to Create a Quilt* on pages 14-17 to quilt, square and trim, then add binding to finish your project.

5A

1. Join 20 blades to make a Dresden plate. Begin sewing at the top of the blade, backstitch, then stop at the bottom. Press all seams to 1 side. Make 3.

2. Fold the 10" light print square in half vertically and horizontally and crease. Center the light square atop a Dresden plate. Using the square as a guide, place a long ruler along 1 edge of the square and trim the Dresden circle. Repeat to trim along the other side of the square. Move the sides out of the way and trim the top and bottom.

3. Cut a 2½" pieced strip from the long edge of each piece you just trimmed. Keep the strips next to their coinciding fabrics on the 10" center unit.

4. Sew a 1½" x 10" sashing rectangle to the top and bottom of the unit. Sew the coinciding pieced strip to the top and bottom. Press.

5. Sew a 1½" x 16" sashing rectangle to both sides of the unit. Press. Line up the center seams and sew the coinciding pieced strips to both sides of the unit. Press. Trim the ends of the pieced strips even with the top and bottom. Make 3.

CHECKERED DRESDEN BED RUNNER

A new variation on a classic pattern. By cutting Dresdens from a strip set, you can create a beautiful runner with a truly amazing look. Our cutting method gives you variations that checkerboard when you turn and assemble them into plates. It's so simple, and comes together so quickly, we know you'll be pleased and proud when you finish it.

materials

PROJECT SIZE
94" x 29½"

- 1 roll of 2½" print strips
- 3¼ yards of background fabric
  - includes center circles and border
- ¾ yard of binding
- 3 yards of backing fabric
  - vertical seam(s) or 1 yard of backing fabric 108" wide
- Missouri Star Large Dresden Plate Template for 10" Squares (template on page 211)
- ¼ yard of Heat n Bond Feather Lite Fusible Interfacing

Checkered Dresden Bed Runner

STEP 1: CUT

From the background fabric, cut:
- (4) 22" strips across the width of the fabric.
  - Subcut (1) 22" square from each strip.
  - From 1 remaining partial strip, subcut (4) 4½" squares.
  - Set the remainders of the strips aside for another project.

STEP 2: MAKE STRIP SETS

From 20* different 2½" print strips, sew 4 strips together to make a strip set. **Make 5**.

Set the remaining print strips aside for another project.

Note: For a scrappier look, cut all 40 print strips in half and use 40 of those to sew strip sets. The remaining half-strips can be set aside for another project.

STEP 3: CUT

From each strip set, cut 18 blades using the Dresden template. Align the 8½" mark on the template with the top of the strip set. As you cut, flip the template 180° to get more pieces per strip. You will need a **total of 80** blades. **3A**

STEP 4: SEW

Fold a Dresden blade in half lengthwise, right sides facing. Sew across the wide end of the folded blade. Clip the corner and turn the blade right side out. Poke the corner out and press with the seam in the center. Repeat to **make 80** blades. **4A**

Select 20 blades and sew them together along the long sides to form a Dresdan plate. Backstitch at the outside edge of each seam. Press. **Make 4** Dresden plates. **4B**

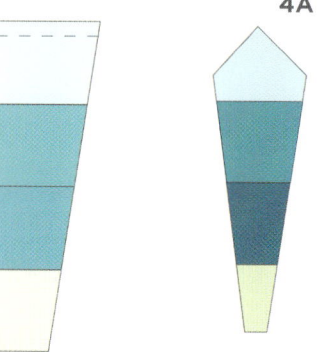

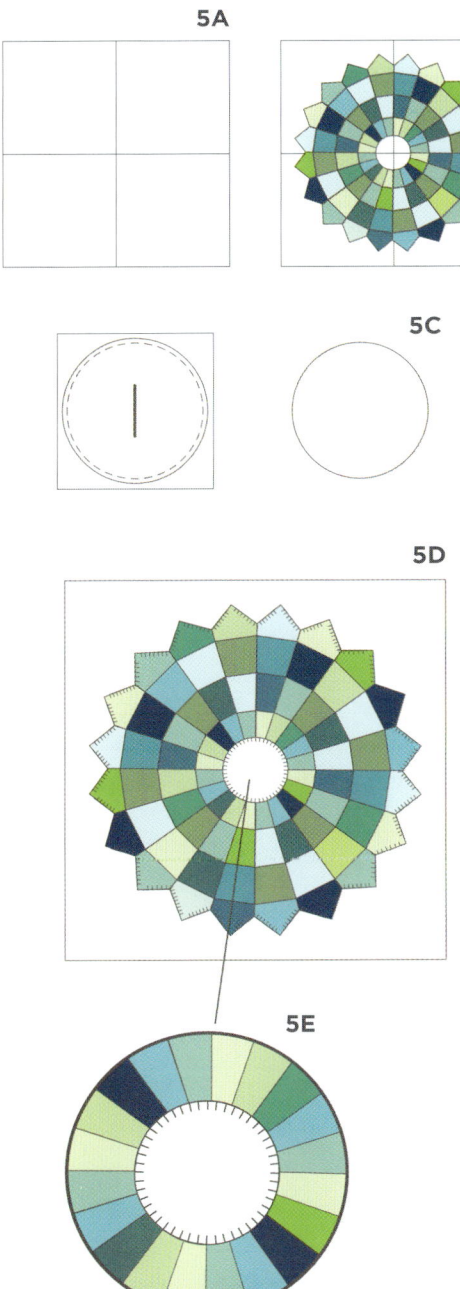

STEP 5: APPLIQUÉ

Fold a 22" background square in half vertically and again horizontally. Lightly press the creases in place. **5A**

Lay a Dresden plate on top of the square, lining up horizontal and vertical seams with the creases in the background square. Pin in place. **5B**

Refer to *Put Your Own Spin On It* on page 22 to find the perfect 4-4½" circle for your project. Use the object to trace a circle onto the fusible interfacing. Cut a slit in the center of the circle.

Place the fusible interfacing circle onto a 4½" square with right sides facing. (The bumpy side of the interfacing will face the right side of the fabric.) Sew ¼" inside of the drawn circle, then trim on the drawn line. Turn the circle right side out, smoothing the edges as you turn so the piece will lie flat. *Do not press!* **5C**

Fuse the circle to the center of the Dresden Plate as shown. Appliqué the circle and Dresden Plate in place using a zigzag or blanket stitch. **Make 4**. **5D 5E**

Block Size: 22" unfinished, 21½" finished

STEP 6: ARRANGE & SEW

Refer to diagram **6A** on the right to arrange the blocks in **1 column of 4**. Once you are happy with the arrangement, sew the blocks together. Press to complete the bed runner.

STEP 7: BORDER

Cut (6) 4½" strips across the width of the background fabric. Sew them together to make 1 long strip. Trim the borders from this strip. Measure, cut, and attach the borders to the project top.

Note: The top and bottom strips are sewn on first. The approximate lengths are 86½" for the sides and 30" for the top and bottom.

STEP 8: QUILT & BIND

Refer to the finishing sections of *How to Create a Quilt* on pages 14-17 to quilt, square and trim, then add binding to finish your project.

6A

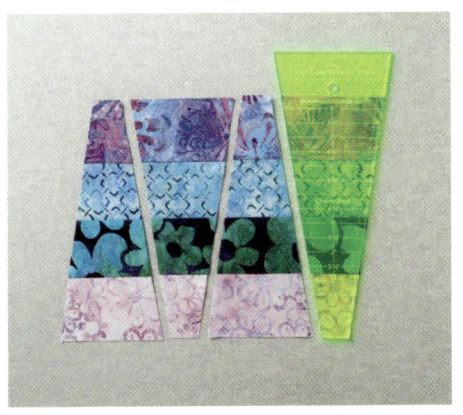

1. Align the 8½″ mark on the Dresden Plate Template on the top of a strip set. Flip the template 180° with each cut to make the most of the fabric.

2. Fold each blade in half with right sides facing and sew across the top. Turn the piece right side out.

3. After sewing and trimming the fusible interfacing to the piece being used for the center of the Dresden Plate, cut a slit in the interfacing and turn right side out.

4. Press the circle to the center of the Dresden Plate and appliqué in place using a blanket stitch.

IMPROV DRESDEN GEESE

Doesn't this gorgeous pattern look just like a flock of geese heading south in formation? The improv method to make these geese is fun and scrappy, and the Dresden template cleans up the edges to stitch your flock together. Set your Dresdens free with this one of a kind project!.

materials

PROJECT SIZE
25" x 14½"

- (3) 10" print squares
- ¼ yard of accent fabric - includes inner half-circle
- 1 yard of background fabric
- ¼ yard of binding fabric
- 1 yard of backing

- Missouri Star 10" paper piecing squares
- Missouri Star Large Dresden Plate Template for 10" Squares (template on page 211)
- ¼ yard of Heat n Bond Lite
- Water soluble glue stick - optional
- Basting spray - optional

THIS QUILT IS INSPIRED BY A MISSOURI STAR TRIPLE PLAY!

Open Camera, Scan Code, Watch Natalie make her Improv Dresden Geese quilt!

Improv Dresden Geese

STEP 1: CUT

From the (3) 10" solid squares, cut (4) 2½" strips across the width of each square for a **total of 12**.

From the accent fabric:
- Cut (1) 5" strip across the width of the fabric.
  - Subcut (1) 5" square.

  - Trim (1) 2½" strip across the width of the remainder of the strip.

  - Set the remainder of the fabric aside for another project.

From the background fabric:
- Cut (1) 15" strip across the width of the fabric.
  - Subcut (1) 15" x 25½" rectangle.

- Cut (6) 2½" strips across the width of the fabric.

- Set the remaining fabric aside for another project.

Use the template to cut 3 Dresden blades from each of 3 paper piecing squares and 1 Dresden blade from 1 paper piecing square for a **total of 10**. **1A**

From the Heat n Bond Lite, cut (1) 4¾" strip across the fusible web. Subcut (1) 4¾" square from the strip.

1A

STEP 2: MAKE THE IMPROV GEESE

Tips: These blocks use a paper piecing method. Set your machine stitch length to 2.0 mm or shorter to prevent tearing out stitches when you remove the paper. It is helpful to have a small cutting mat, rotary cutter, small ironing mat, and iron close to your sewing machine.

Fold a paper blade in half lengthwise and crease to mark the center. **2A**

Select a 2½″ accent strip and cut a section at least as wide as the bottom of the blade. Apply a small amount of glue to the bottom of the paper and adhere the print piece to the paper right side up. **Note**: If you are not using glue, you may wish to sew a couple basting stitches across the print piece and paper, approximately ⅛″ from the bottom edges. **2B**

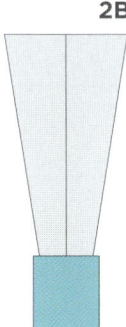

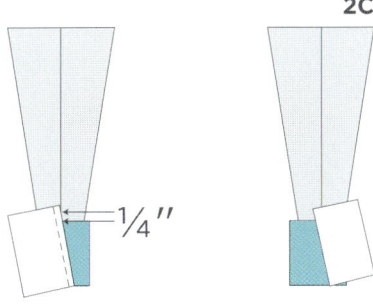

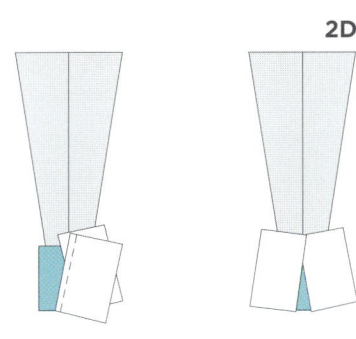

From a 2½" background strip, cut a piece approximately 3" long. Lay the background piece, right side down, on an angle, as shown. The top edge of the background piece should meet the center crease approximately ¼" above the accent piece and the bottom corner of the background piece should be just inside the edge of the blade. Sew along the angled edge. Press the background piece over the seam. **2C**

Repeat to add another background piece to the opposite side as shown. **2D**

Turn the unit over and carefully trim along the edges of the paper. **2E**

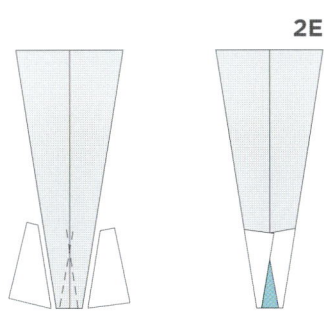

STEP 2: MAKE THE IMPROV GEESE (CONTINUED)

From a 2½" solid strip, cut a piece the width of the Dresden blade approximately ½" above the crossing point of the sewn accent piece. Lay the print piece face down, below the sewn background pieces. Sew across the top of the solid piece. Press over the seam. **2F**

Repeat as before with (2) 2½" background pieces to make another "goose." **2G**

In the same manner, add 2 more geese to your Dresden blade, cutting the print pieces the width of the blade after each goose. **2H**

Remove the paper backing. Fold the blade in half lengthwise, right sides together. Sew across the wide end of the folded blade. Trim the folded corner to reduce the bulk and turn the blade right side out. Gently poke out the corner. Press, centering the seam. Repeat the instructions to fold, sew, trim, turn, and press each blade. **Make 10**. **2I**

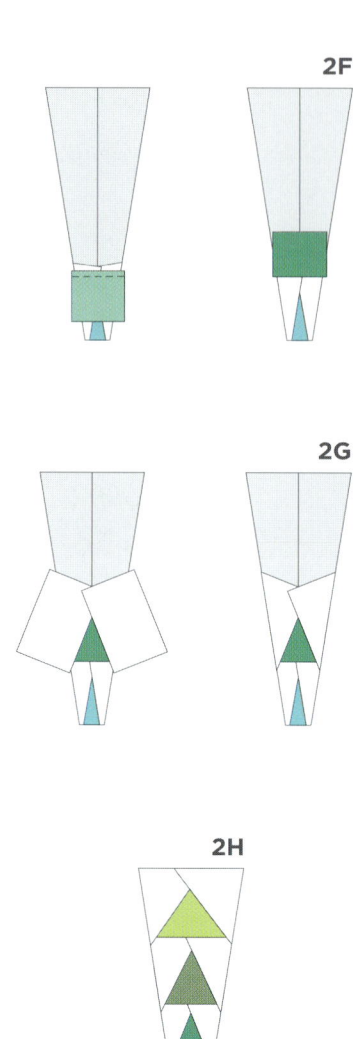
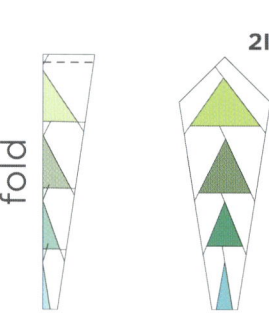

3A

STEP 3: BLOCK CONSTRUCTION

Sew the blades together as shown to make a Dresden fan. Press. **3A**

3B

Fold the 15″ x 25½″ background rectangle in half and crease to mark the center. Lay the Dresden fan on top of the square, aligning the bottom edges, and the matching centers of the fan and rectangle. Use the basting spray as directed or pin as needed to hold the fan in place. **3B**

3C

Refer to *Put Your Own Spin On It* on page 22 to find the perfect 4½″ circle for your project. Use the object to trace a circle onto the paper side of the Heat n Bond square. Following the manufacturer's instructions, fuse the adhesive web square to the wrong side of the 5″ acccent square. Cut on the traced line. Fold the fused circle in half. Remove the paper backing and discard it.

Lay the fused circle on top of the bottom edge of the Dresden fan, adhesive side down, and lining up the center crease with the center of the rectangle. When you are happy with your placement, pin the circle in place, and trim along the bottom edge even with the block. Carefully remove the pins and fuse the circle according to the manufacturer's instructions. **3C**

3D

Use a blanket or zigzag stitch to appliqué the half-circle and fan in place around the outer edges. **3D**

Block Size: 25½″ x 15″ unfinished, 25″ x 14½″ finished

STEP 4: QUILT & BIND

Layer the project with batting and backing then quilt. Refer to the finishing sections of *How to Create a Quilt* on pages 14-17 to quilt, square and trim, then add binding to finish your project. **4A**

4A

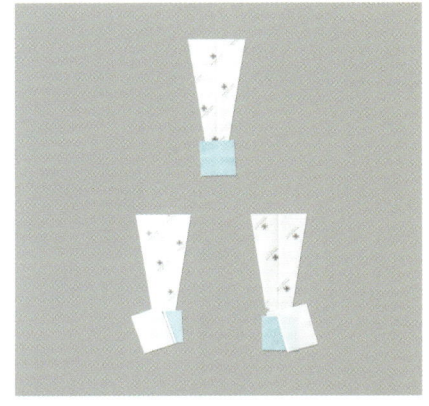 
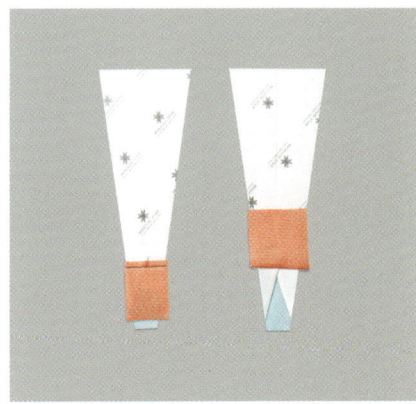 

1. Apply a small amount of glue to the bottom of the paper and adhere the accent piece to the paper right side up. Lay a 3" background piece, right side down, on an angle, as shown. Sew along the angled edge. Press the background piece over the seam.

2. Repeat to add another background piece to the opposite side as shown. Turn the unit over and trim along the edges of the paper.

3. Cut a solid piece the width of the Dresden blade approximately ½" above the crossing point of the sewn background pieces. Lay the solid piece face down, below the sewn background pieces. Sew across the top of the print piece. Press over the seam.

4. Repeat as before with (2) 2½" background pieces to make another "goose."

5. In the same manner, add 2 more geese to your Dresden blade, cutting the solid pieces the width of the blade for each goose.

6. Remove the paper backing. Fold the blade in half lengthwise, right sides together. Sew across the wide end of the folded blade. Trim the folded corner to reduce the bulk and turn the blade right side out. Gently poke out the corner. Press, centering the seam. Make 10.

DRESDEN MAGIC —TIPS & TRICKS—

So versatile… so classic… so fun! The Dresden blade is a classic shape that gives quilters a great number of possibilities. As you'll find throughout this book, you are not confined to one type of Dresden quilt. Instead, we'll teach you how to achieve wildly different results from a few simple techniques.

When Dresden blades are sewn together to form a complete circle, this creates a full Dresden Plate. You'll find this traditional quilt block in many contemporary and vintage patterns. But, partial Dresden Plates show up in traditional patterns, too! As Dresden quilts have skewed more modern, they often incorporate just part of the Dresden Plate—either quarter, half, or three-quarter portions. Throughout this book, we are going to teach you some "magic tricks" to use on Dresden blocks, which you can use to change their appearance.

CUTTING MAGIC

Sometimes, we shave off the edge of a Dresden fan in order to piece it into a quilt. Now, that's some Dresden magic! You'll see an example of this technique din the *Dresden Squared Runner* on page 154. We'll teach you how to center the block with your ruler and trim off the appropriate amount. It's easier than you think! You can use this same trimming technique on quarter plates to square up a block and piece it into a quilt. To use a squaring ruler effectively, you'll want to center the ruler's 45° angle line with the Dresden blade that's in the middle of your quarter fan.

Speaking of cutting magic, did you know you can cut Dresden blades from different parts of the template to make petals of different widths? Check out the *Bloom and Grow* project on page 112 for an example of how you can pair long and skinny blades with chunky blades to make an assortment of Dresden plate flowers!

PIECING MAGIC

Oftentimes, we use patchwork to make Dresden blades more fancy. For instance, we love piecing strip sets from jelly rolls and cutting Dresden blades from the resulting patchwork fabrics. It's fast to piece but looks so intricate! Watch the magic that happens when you mix up the blades in random order; see *Checkered Dresden Bed Runner* (page 164). And if you are looking for more of a challenge, we invite you to flex your improvisational piecing muscles with The *Improv Dresden Geese* on page 172.

FOLDING MAGIC

If you've worked with Dresdens before, you know that little bit of magic that happens when you fold the blade in half, sew across the top, and press it into a point. But what happens when you give the blade bottoms the same treatment? Find out in our *Dresden Wreath* project on page 104. We also use fold lines to help us center our appliquéd fans onto background blocks and floral centers just right. Before centering your appliqués, first fold and press the background blocks and circle appliqués in half, and use the crease to place your Dresden plates and fans! Check out *Here Comes the Sun* (page 52) and the other Dresden quilts in this book for more cutting, piecing, and folding magic.

IMPROVISING SEAMS

Can we let you in on a little secret? Sometimes our Dresden seams are a little too scant or a bit too wide, causing the blades to have an odd fit. It's all good! For seams that are a little too scant, we just take a second seam a few threads in. This can make all the difference to a plate or partial plate to make it lay flatter on the quilt. If you notice your seams have been too wide and you're running out of blades, it's okay to improvise and switch to a thinner seam as you add on the final few sections. The resulting block will still be gorgeous, and nobody has to know about the secret behind your seams.

Making Shapes with Dresdens

So, what else can the classic Dresden fan do? As you play with Dresdens and see what different shapes are possible, you'll likely want to start layering the blades on top of one another to make new and intriguing shapes. We'll teach you to make seasonal favorites like Christmas trees and Thanksgiving turkeys, plus modern motifs like flower vases and succulents throughout the projects in this book.

What other shapes can you build with Dresden blades? Remember, we're dealing with folded fabrics, sometimes on top of other folded fabrics. As you attempt to stitch through all those layers, just keep these tips in mind and it will be smooth sailing!

1. SEW ONE LAYER AT A TIME.

It's tempting to want to place all your layers and sew them to the background at the same time. We get it! However, for the best results, we recommend smoothing out and sewing down the bottom layer first. Then, you can place and stitch down the next layer. Stitching down one layer at a time can help keep your blades from shifting, and it also gives you some sneakier options for hiding thread tails. We also think going one row at a time makes it more comfortable to lift the presser foot and pivot on your sewing machine.

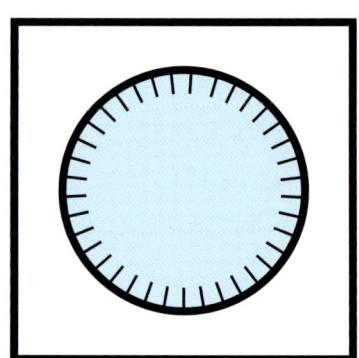

2. CHANGE YOUR NEEDLE.

How many Dresden blades can you layer on top of one another? Believe it or not, your sewing machine can handle a lot! (Just ask anyone who has accidentally sewn through a finger.) When sewing through thick layers, we recommend swapping in a Microtex (sharp) needle to get the job done. A stiletto tool or pointer helps hold down the points and keeps your fingers out of harm's way. Don't be shy about using your sewing machine's needle down function if you have it, or you can turn the handwheel to lower the needle down manually.

3. GO SLOWLY.

There's no need to rush as you sew down those Dresden points or add layers upon layers. If you can manually adjust your machine's speed, take it down a notch and enjoy the slow and steady rhythm of the needle. You can take a few stitches at a time as you glide around curves and tack down points. (See our tips in *All About Dresden Appliqué* on page 88).

4. HAVE FUN!

Making shapes from Dresdens can be a very relaxing and organic experience. As you think about trees, plants, and botanicals, remember that nature is perfectly imperfect. Relax and let the fabric guide you. Perhaps you can take a cue from painter Bob Ross, who famously said, "We don't make mistakes, just happy little accidents." The natural variants in trees and plants give them character, so let these imperfections shine.

The same goes for wreaths and layered florals. As you sew these to your background blocks, feel free to let loose and have fun! If you choose not to follow the folded guidelines on your background squares, it's find thinner seam as you add on the final few sections. The resulting block will still be gorgeous, and nobody has to know about the secret behind your seams.

Regardless of your prior quilting experience, we want to empower you and Dresdens are incredibly fun, beginner-friendly, and versatile blocks to play with. Watch our tutorials on YouTube to see how Jenny, Natalie, and Misty find the techniques that work for them. We know you'll discover a new trick or two that will help you on your way. And we sincerely hope that you'll love Dresdens as much as we do!

WATCH OUR TIPS AND TRICKS IN ACTION.

Open Camera, Scan Code, Watch our Dresden tutorials on YouTube!

ALL IN A ROW AND ALL IN A ROLL PILLOWS

An attractive throw pillow can really tie a room together—sometimes even better than a good rug. By alternating your Dresdens to form a straight or circular design you can create a wonderful little decor accessory that really finishes off a space. All is well, when you go all in, and end up with a truly stunning pillows.

materials

ALL IN A ROW PILLOW SIZE 22" x 15"	ALL IN A ROLL PILLOW SIZE 22" circle
• (11) 10" print squares*	• 1 large coordinating shanked button
• ½ yard of backing fabric for All in a Row pillow - includes border strips	• 1 yard of backing
• ¾ yard of backing fabric for All in a Roll pillow - includes center circle	• Missouri Star Large Dresden Plate Template for 10" Squares (template on page 211)
• ¾ yard of background fabric	*Enough Dresden blades can be cut from (11) 10" print squares for both pillows. You may choose to use more 10" print squares for greater variety.*
• Polyester fiberfill	
• 5" Square of Heat n Bond	

All In A Row and All In A Roll Pillows

1A

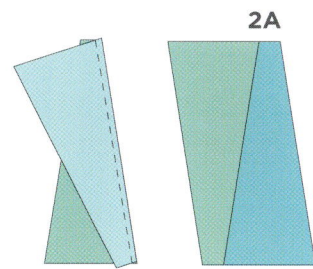
2A

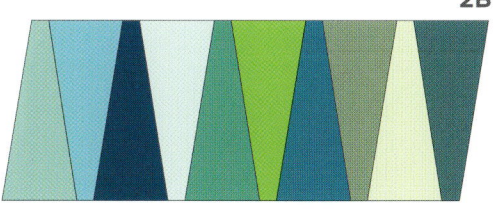
2B

STEP 1: SELECT & CUT

From each of the (11) 10" print squares, cut 3 blades using the template. Each square will yield 3 pieces and a **total of 31** are needed if you chose to make the pillows exactly like the ones shown. **1A**

Set aside a **total of 11** blades for the All in a Row Pillow. Set aside a **total of 20** blades for the All in a Roll Pillow.

pillow 1 – all in a row

STEP 2: PILLOW FRONT

The front panel consists of a row of 10 blades sewn side-by-side, 2 half-blades and 2 strips framing the row lengthwise.

Start by sewing blades together to create a row. Alternate the blade orientation: down, up, down, up. Right sides facing, offset the wedges at the ¼" seam allowance matching wide to narrow sides. Sew 10 together. Press. **2A 2B**

STEP 3: ENDS

Use the Dresden template to cut 1 Dresden blade in half. These halves will complete the row and make a rectangle. Line up the template's center line with 1 side of the blade. Make sure the template and the blade are pointing in the same direction. Cut. **3A**

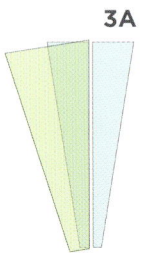

Attach these half-blades to the ends of the row. Be careful to sew along the angled edge—you want the straight side of the half-blade to finish the row. Press. **3B**

STEP 4: TOP & BOTTOM

Cut (2) 3½" strips of backing fabric. Measure the length of the Dresden row and subcut the strip to that size, approximately 22½". **Make 2**.

Attach 1 strip to the top; the other to the bottom of the Dresden row. Press to the strips. Topstitch about ⅛" from the seam on each strip. **4A**

STEP 5: PILLOW BACK

Use the completed pillow front as a pattern to cut a back piece from the yardage.

Place the front and the back together with right sides facing. **5A**

With pins, mark about a 7" opening on 1 of the short ends. Start by backstitching at a pin; sew all the way around the pillow using a ¼" seam allowance. Backstitch again as you reach the second pin. **5B**

Clip the corners. Turn right side out. Push the corners out. Press. At the opening, turn the seam allowance to the inside and hold it taut as you press.

STEP 6: FINISHING

Use polyester stuffing to fill the pillow. With needle and thread, close the opening using an invisible stitch.

All in a Row Pillow Size: 15½" x 22"

pillow 2 – all in a roll

STEP 7: SEW

Take the 20 blades set aside earlier and sew them together—matching wide ends. Press. **7A**

STEP 8: PILLOW CENTER

From the backing fabric, cut (1) 5" square from 1 corner of the fabric.

Refer to *Put Your Own Spin On It* on page 22 to find the perfect 4½-5" circle for your project. Use the object to trace a circle onto the paper side of the Heat n Bond square **8A**.

Follow the manufacturer's instructions to adhere the Heat n Bond square to the reverse side of the 5" backing square. Cut on the line and discard the paper backing.

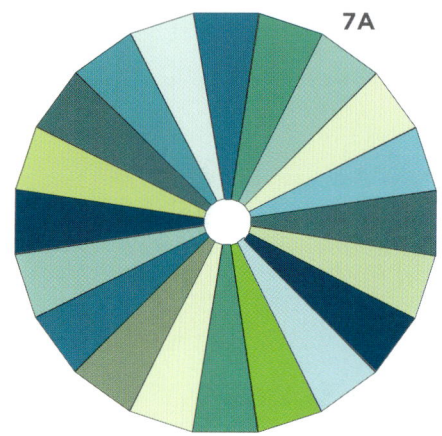

7A

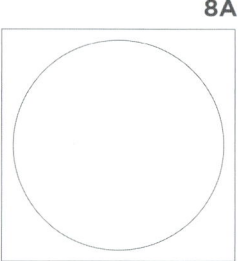

8A

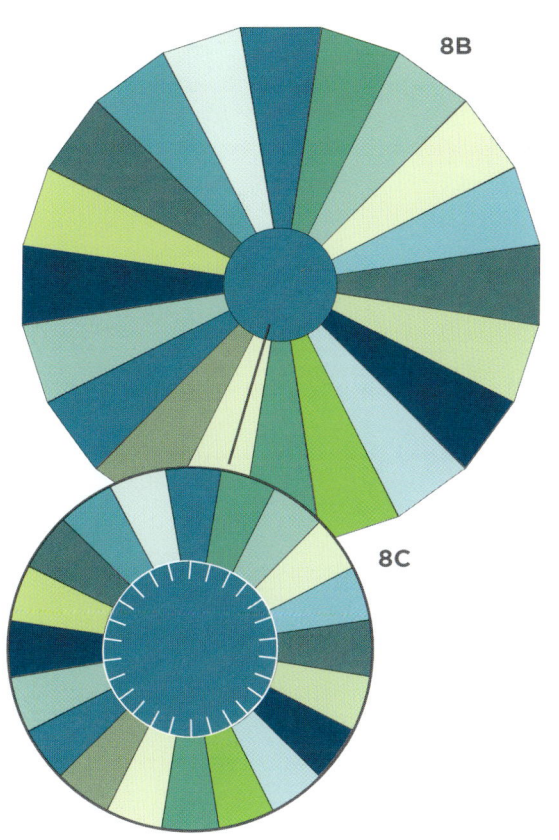

Lay paper underneath the hole of your Dresden circle to protect your ironing surface from the adhesive. Lay the center circle atop the hole. When you are happy with your placement, follow the manufacturer's instructions to adhere in place. **8B**

Stitch along the edge of the circle using a straight, zigzag, blanket or satin stitch. **8C**

STEP 9: PILLOW BACK

Use the pillow top as a pattern to cut the backing fabric.

Layer the backing circle and pillow top right sides facing. Stitch around the perimeter using a ¼" seam allowance. Leave a 4"-6" opening. Backstitch on both sides of the opening. **9A**

STEP 10: STUFF & SEW

Turn the pillow right sides out. Fill the pillow with stuffing. Close the opening by handstitching. Turn the seam allowances toward the inside as you slipstitch, catching the folded edges with your needle.

STEP 11: ATTACH THE BUTTON

Mark the center of the circle before sewing the button in place. Use a heavy, waxed thread or doubled up strands of embroidery floss.

Knot the thread and draw it up from the back of the pillow to the front. Thread the needle through the shank of the button, attaching it to the fabric until you feel it's secure. Pull the needle and thread back through the pillow to the back and up to the top several times, pulling the thread taut.

When you feel the button is secure, knot the thread and pull the knot through the fabric to bury it inside the pillow. Trim the thread close to the fabric while it is pulled taut. The tail end of the thread will sink into the inside of the pillow.

All in a Roll Pillow Size: 22" circle

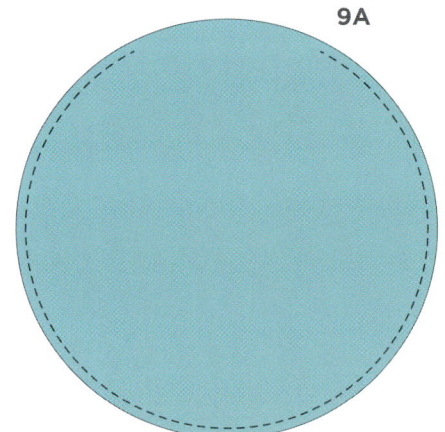

9A

 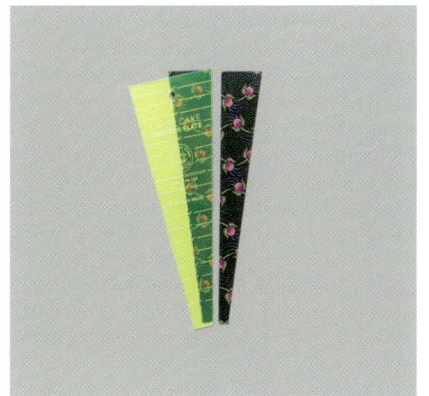

1. Start by sewing blades together to create a row. Alternate the blade orientation: down, up, down, up. Right sides facing, offset the wedges at the ¼" seam allowance matching wide to narrow sides. Sew 10 together. Press.

2. Line up the template's center line with 1 side of the Dresden blade and cut in half. Make sure the template and the blade are pointing in the same direction.

3. Attach these half-blades to the ends of the row. Be careful to sew along the angled edge—you want the straight side of the half-blade to finish the row. Press.

4. Cut (2) 3½" strips of backing fabric. Attach 1 strip to the top; the other to the bottom of the Dresden row. Press to the strips. Topstitch about ⅛" from the seam on each strip.

5. Take the 20 blades set aside earlier and sew them together—matching wide ends. Press.

6. Lay paper underneath the hole of your Dresden circle to protect your ironing surface from the adhesive. Lay the center circle atop the hole. When you are happy with your placement, follow the manufacturer's instructions to adhere in place.

SPARE CHANGE BAG

This cute little bag is perfect for holding your loose change, extra jewelry, or a backup set of sewing scissors. By sewing some Dresdens together in an almost half-circle, you can put together this fun and useful project in no time! It's so much fun, you'll spare no expense! Pull out that favorite fabric you've been holding onto for this fun accessory!

materials

- 1 package of 10" print sqares
- ¾ yard complimentary print fabric - for lining and handles
- 2 yards Pellon Shape Flex 101 Fusible Woven Interfacing
- Missouri Star Large Dresden Plate Template for 10" Squares (template on page 211)

Spare Change Bag

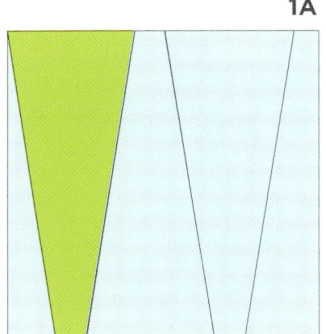

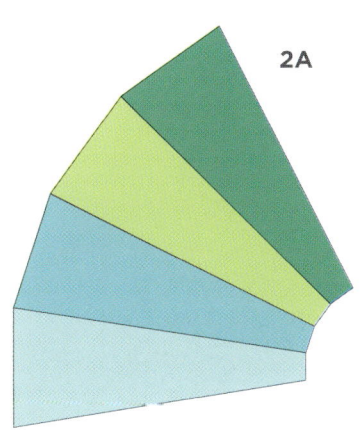

STEP 1: SELECT & CUT

Use the Dresden template to cut a **total of 22** blades. Each side of the bag consists of 11 blades. It's up to you if you'd like to use all different fabrics or just a few repeated. Each square will yield 3 blades. **1A**

STEP 2: OUTER PANELS

Sew 4 blades together with the small ends all together. Press. **Make 4**. **2A**

Arrange (2) 4-blade sections and 3 blades as shown. Sew the units together. Press. **Make 2**. **2B**

STEP 3: TRIM

Use the template to trim the ends of both panels. Line up the template's center line with the last sewn seam as shown. Cut. **3A**

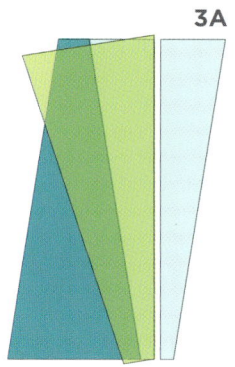

STEP 4: CUT

Use the outer panels as patterns. Cut out interfacing for each. Follow the manufacturer's instructions to adhere the interfacing to the reverse side of each panel. Make sure the bumpy texture is against the fabric. **4A**

From the lining fabric cut a 4½" strip across the width of fabric and set aside for the handles. Again use the outer panels as patterns, but this time cut 1 lining panel for each outer panel. These are the inner panels. **4B**

Next use the lining as a pattern and cut interfacing for both lining pieces. Follow the manufacturer's instructions to adhere interfacing to each lining.

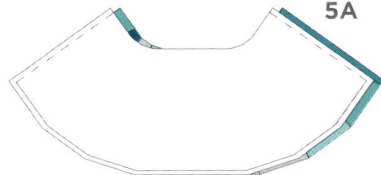

STEP 5: SEW OUTER PANELS

With the outer fabric panels right sides together, sew both sides and the bottom closed. Backstitch at the begining and end. **5A**

To form the gussets, open the seam flat and match the side to the bottom seam at the corner. From the corner's tip, mark 2" down the center and at 3" on the folded sides. Use a pencil to connect those points. Sew along this line backstitching at the beginning and end. **5B**

Trim to a ¼". Turn right side out. Gently push out corners.

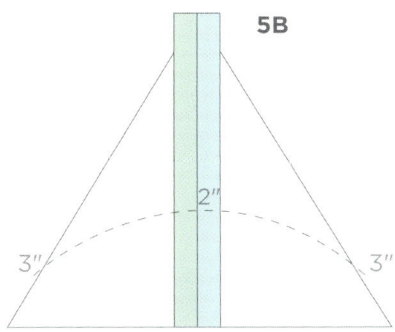

STEP 6: HANDLES

Use the 4½" strip cut from the lining fabric to make bag handles. Remove the selvages and cut (2) 20" strips. Fold in half lengthwise and press. Open up and fold both sides into the center fold. Press. Close the first fold again so there are four layers. **6A**

Topstitch about ⅛" along both lengthwise edges. **6B**

One handle is positioned onto each outer panel. Place the raw ends of the handle along the top edge of the outer panel. Align the inner fold of the handle to either side of the center wedge. Be careful not to twist it as you put it in place. Stitch ¼" from the top edge to secure the handles in place. **6C**

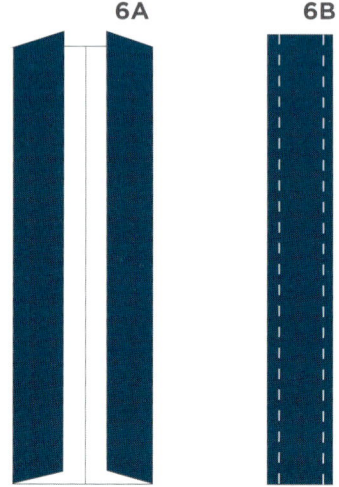

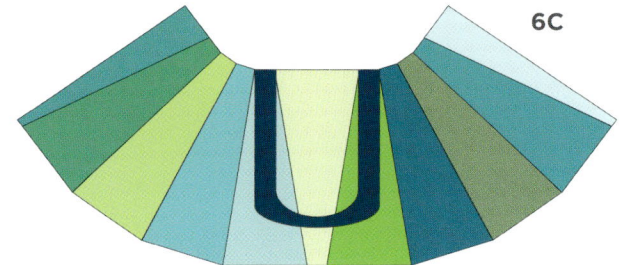

STEP 7: LINING

Sew the lining together in the same manner as the purse panels except this time leave a 4" opening along the bottom for turning. **7A**

Make the gussets as in **5B**. Do not turn the lining inside out.

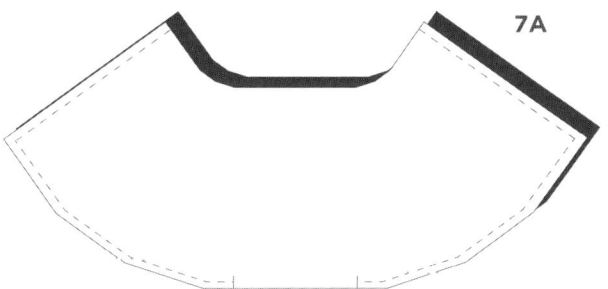

7A

STEP 8: SEW TOGETHER

Set the completed outer panel of the bag inside the lining that is still wrong side out. They should be right sides together. Push the handles down between the 2 layers keeping them out of the way. Match raw edges along the top opening. Make sure to line up the side seams. Pin together and sew ½" seam all around the top.

Pull bag through the opening in the lining.

STEP 9: FINISHING

To permanently close the opening, tuck the seam allowances to the inside and tug both sides of the hole. Press along the folds that are created. At the sewing machine topstitch along the fold close to the edge. Make sure to backstitch at both ends. Push the lining into the bag pushing out the sides and bottom. Pull the handles up.

Roll the lining at the top opening slightly to the inside, press, then topstitch ⅛" from the top edge. **9A**

9A

1 To make the gusset, line up the bottom and side seams of the bag.

2 On each side of the gusset mark 3" on the fold.

3 Mark 2" down the center of the seam.

4 Insert the outer bag inside the lining, right sides together.

5 After turning the bag right side out, gently push out the gusset. See how the bottom and side seams match.

6 To close the opening, fold the seam allowances in and tug at either side. Press and topstitch very close to the folded edge backstitching at both ends.

TEMPLATES

DRESDEN
TREE STAR

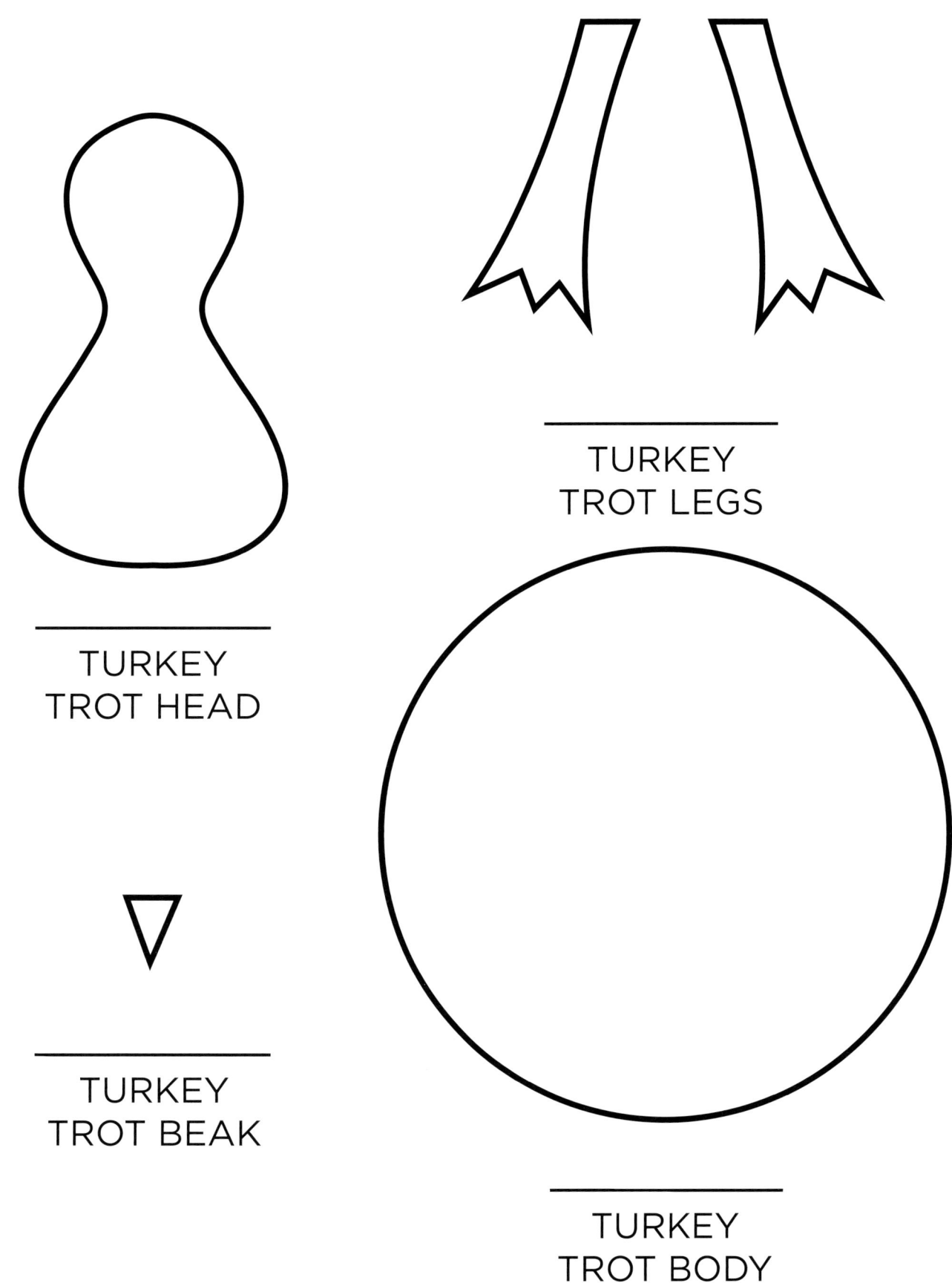

TEMPLATES

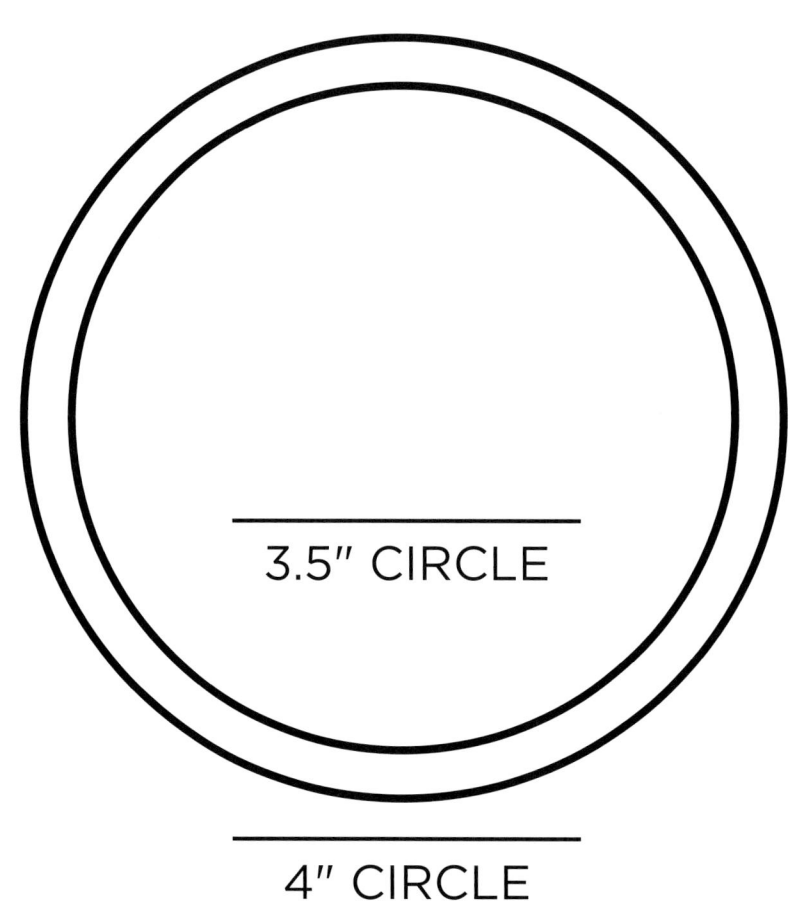

3.5" CIRCLE

4" CIRCLE

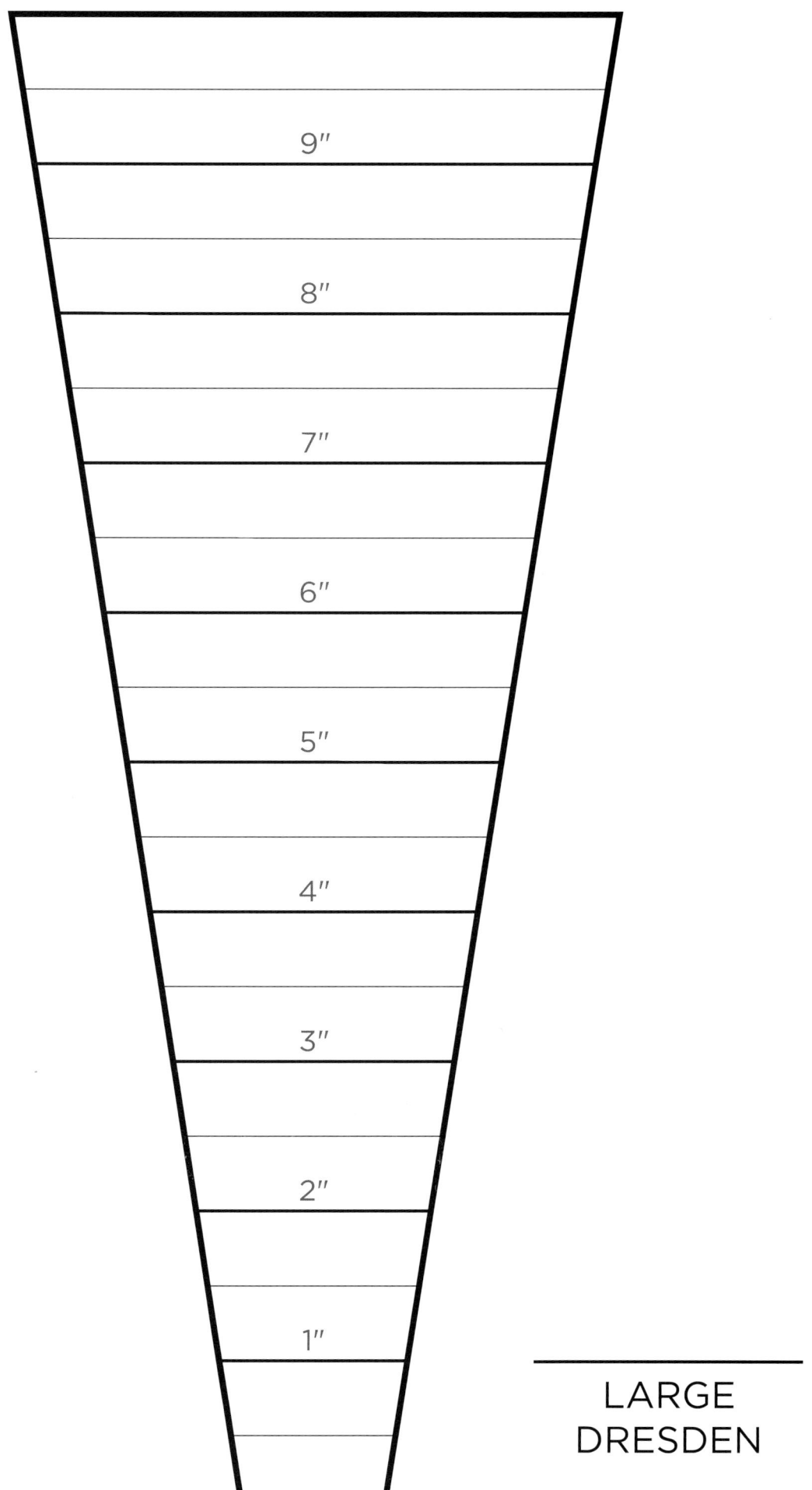

REFERENCE - *Articles*

08
DISCOVER SIMPLY BEAUTIFUL DRESDENS

10
HOW TO CREATE A QUILT

20
USING PRECUTS

22
PUT YOUR OWN SPIN ON IT

88
ALL ABOUT DRESDEN APPLIQUÉ

150
MAKING DRESDEN BORDER STRIPS

182
DRESDEN MAGIC TIPS & TRICKS

208
TEMPLATES

REFERENCE - *Patterns*

26 - DRESDEN BOTANICA

34 - MINI SUNFLOWER PILLOW

44 - GRANDMOTHER'S FAN

52 - HERE COMES THE SUN

60 - FANCY DRESDEN FANS

68 - TINY DRESDENS

76- TURKEY TROT

94 - DRESDEN TREE WALL HANGING

104 - DRESDEN WREATH WALL HANGING

REFERENCE - *Patterns*

112 - BLOOM AND GROW WALL HANGING

124 - SPRING DRESDENS TABLE RUNNER

134 - JOSH'S STAR

142 - DRESDEN COIN

154 - DRESDEN SQUARED TABLE RUNNER

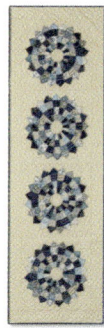
164 - CHECKERED DRESDEN BED RUNNER

172 - IMPROV DRESDEN GEESE WALL HANGING

188 - ALL IN A ROW & ALL IN A ROLL PILLOWS

198 - SPARE CHANGE BAG